THE
STAINED
GLASS
HANDBOOK

THE
STAINED
GLASS
HANDBOOK

Viv Foster

Grange BOOKS

AN OCEANA BOOK

Published by Grange Books
an imprint of Grange Books Plc
The Grange
Kingsnorth Industrial Estate
Hoo, nr. Rochester
Kent ME3 9ND
www.grangebooks.co.uk

ISBN 1-84013-904-8

This book was produced by
Quantum Books
6 Blundell Street
London N7 9BH

QUMSGH2

Manufactured in Singapore by
Universal Graphics Pte Ltd
Printed in China by
CT Printing Ltd

Contents

Introduction

Stained glass is actually an accepted misnomer of words to describe all coloured and painted glass used in a decorative way. In reality there are two distinct types of "stained glass" that bear a resemblance to one another but, in fact, are quite different. The delicate figures seen in church windows are really quite separate from the Tiffany-style glass lampshades found in bars, restaurants and private homes.

This book aims to focus on the main skills and offer readers the opportunity to learn a basic, working knowledge of each technique. By supplying a basic framework, it is our hope that the creativity in you will flourish and discover a means of new expression.

In reality, any work that relies solely on the innate qualities of coloured glass could be more accurately described as "glass art". Stained glass should refer only to coloured or plain glass that has been painted, decorated or further processed by the artists themselves. However, the term itself is now so widely accepted that "stained glass" is understood to encompass everything from a simple coloured glass window ornament to a magnificently stained and painted church window.

TOP *The intricacy of a curved Tiffany-style shade fascinates many people, but they are made from small pieces of flat glass assembled over a curved form.*

RIGHT *This is a glorious example of leaded work using fragments of hand-painted Victorian glass that the artist collected during a period as a glass restorer.*

A Short History of Glass

The likely origins of glass are believed to emanate from the Egyptians, where glass was possibly first used as jewellery. From Egypt the use of glass radiated outward to Byzantium and then to Greece and Rome.

ABOVE *An excellent example of early domestic stained glass, this Victorian roundel shows craftsmen at work.*

It is known from the excavations of Herculaneum and Pompeii that the Romans were the first to use glass as a window by placing pieces in the openings of their stonework. The craft developed and in time, glass-blowing replaced molding. Technical skills improved and glass became transparent as opposed to translucent. The influence of the glass worker eventually found its way to France where stained glass windows as we know them today first developed. Throughout the Middle Ages, stained glass was an ecclestiastical art form that helped to educate a largely illiterate population in the stories of the Bible. It is possible that the earliest known stained glass windows are those in the Augesburg Cathedral in Germany and date from the 11th century. The famous windows of Chartres in France and Canterbury and York, to name but a few, came later.

The high point for these medieval windows was around the 13th and 14th centuries.

In the 16th century came the rebellion against Rome and commissioned religious work declined dramatically. By royal decree many pieces of fine glass were systematically destroyed as stained glass was considered too ornate and extravagant for the Protestant Church of the time. Not only was this disastrous for the existing stained glass craft but there was yet more trouble for the manufacturers on the European continent who had developed the technique of making coloured glass into a highly specialized industry. Many of the glass houses or producers situated in the Lorraine were destroyed by war in 1633 and the secrets and techniques of glass-making lay buried in the rubble for centuries to come.

The craft now directed itself toward heraldic and domestic windows and there came a period when clear or white glass as it is now known was painted with enamels.

In place of the richly coloured medieval windows, which had transmitted light, the new work seemed dull and opaque in comparison.

Fortunately, the 19th-century witnessed a revival and the beauty of stained glass was rediscovered. In 1850, the formula for making medieval coloured glass was reformulated and in the 1860s William Morris revived the medieval expertise by using this new style of coloured glass in his windows. Edward Burne Jones also contributed considerably to popularising stained glass and then these men – among others – designed windows not only for churches but also for domestic settings. Stained glass was once again thriving.

In America, there was also an

ABOVE *The Dawning of The Last Day, by Frederick Ashwin, 1871, is the only recorded work by this stained-glass artist in Britain.*

enormous influence on glass by Louis Comfort Tiffany, who broke away from the traditions of joining glass with lead channels by inventing the copper foil technique. Tiffany, the son of the famous jeweller, is also known for using opalescent glass in his designs, but it was actually John La Farge who obtained the first patent for this revolutionary material in February, 1880.

In the last 20 years there has been a tremendous interest in stained glass as a growing hobby and craft industry. Old window panels are carefully restored to their former glory and new works are commissioned to reflect the architecture of today. Stained glass is seen as both a craft that can be learned as a satisfying hobby and an independent art form.

For those interested in taking up glass as a hobby, there is an ever-increasing wealth of new materials, information and equipment available. This book offers information, techniques and projects to inspire you to explore further.

Constituents of Glass

Early glass was made from common fine sand, whose melting point was lowered by mixing with it a flux such as wood ash. Sand is a form of silica, but quartz crystals or flint can be used as well. Soda ash is now commonly added as a flux, with limestone as a stabilizer, and often unwanted small pieces of glass, known as cullet, are included too.

This mixture melts at about 1,400°C (2,550°F), and when annealed, or cooled, goes from its liquid state to solid glass. As the temperature is slowly dropped, the treacle-like glass can be formed by shaping it for all its many uses.

Roman glass tended to be greenish in colour because of the impurities of the iron oxides in the silica they used. Theophilus, a Benedictine monk, wrote a handbook on the crafts of the time in probably the 12th century. Called Diversarum Artium Schedula, or Diverse Arts, it described, among other things, the making of glass: 'First cut many beechwood logs and dry them out, then burn them all together in a clean place and carefully collect the ashes, taking care that you do not mix any earth or stones with them'. He detailed the building of the kilns, mixing ash with fine sand, placing a clay pot inside the kiln, and then firing until it is melted, and handling the resulting glass when cooled.

The first recorded glassmaker in England was Laurence Vitrearius, literally, Laurence the Glassmaker. He is recorded as working in the first half of the 13th century in the south of the country, where potash produced from bracken

and beechwood served to make a quite different glass from, for instance, that in southern Europe, where soda flux made from the ashes of marie plants was commonly used. The search for the right ingredients to make completely clear glass that was also strong and resisted erosion occupied the makers of glass for many centuries.

Much medieval glass was a result of trial and error, as glassmakers struggled to find the perfect ingredients and their correct proportions. Such experiments often resulted in corrosion of the surface and even gradual disintegration of some glass of this period. In the 16th century in England, Jean Carré from Antwerp was granted a 21-year licence by Elizabeth I to make window glass. In the next century, alarmed at the quantity of wood being cut to make glass and fire the furnaces, James I forbade its use by Royal Decree. The glassmakers then turned to coal as their fuel and glass manufacture moved to the north of the country, where supplies were plentiful and easily mined. Until the 19th century, window glass was taxed as a luxury in Europe and it was not until 1845 that the tax was finally abolished in England.

Early Glassmaking

The very earliest glass manufacture entailed wrapping molten glass around a core of clay or bag of sand. When the glass cooled, the clay could be chipped away or the sand drained out of its bag, leaving a hollow shaped vase or drinking vessel that later was given stability by adding a base on which it could stand upright. These vessels were often decorated, sometimes with colour.

The first use of coloured glass was for beads and other jewellery, and also as an early form of currency. The first attempts at making flat glass by pouring molten glass onto a cooling surface resulted in a pitted and uneven sheet. Clean, clear, flat glass was not produced until the method of glass-blowing was discovered.

Blowing involves the use of a hollow rod to inject air into the melt, and was probably a Syrian invention in the 2nd century B.C. The glassblower dips the rod into a pot of molten glass in the furnace, and takes out a blob known as a gather. By blowing down the tube, air is used to balloon the glass into a bubble. The bubble on the end of the blowing rod is then swung alternately from side to side and blown again, until it becomes elongated. Before the glass solidifies, the ends are cut off, forming a hollow

BELOW *By blowing down the hollow tube, air is used to balloon the glass into a bubble.*

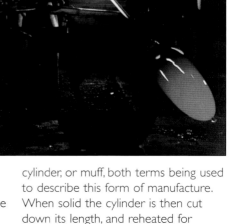

cylinder, or muff, both terms being used to describe this form of manufacture. When solid the cylinder is then cut down its length, and reheated for

flattening and smoothing by a wood block while it is still in the "lehr", or annealing chamber, of the kiln. The final process of cooling must be done slowly to prevent both crystalization and the shattering of the glass. This method of glassmaking is continued today, producing what is called "antique" glass. What results is a sheet of uneven thickness and colour, giving the light coming through it great beauty and subtlety. It is this "antique" glass that is traditionally used for stained glass. Other forms of early glassmaking included casting it and pouring it into molds.

The Introduction of Colour

Coloured glass was in use more than a thousand years before the discovery of how to make transparent, or white, glass.

Coloured glass has a long history, predating the invention of transparent class by a millennium or more. Most probably due to accidents and impurities caused in the production process, it was discovered that certain metallic oxides added to the melt resulted in coloured glass. Certainly by the 5th century A.D., the Romans had found that a little copper dispersed in the melt produced a ruby-coloured glass; medieval glassmakers later discovered a rose-pink colour, and in the 17th century the addition of gold chloride was found to produce a beautiful, rich ruby colour. One of the first glass colours was blue, made by adding minute traces of cobalt or

ABOVE *The cylinder or "muff."*

copper. Green was originally the result of impurities, but later, copper or iron was used.

Many of the ingredients used to produce particular colours or effects remain the manufacturer's secret even today, and the variety of hues possible is almost endless. Glass that is of a strong single colour throughout is called pot-metal glass. Streaky glass has variations of colour, while tints are pale colours. Opaque white glass was originally produced using antimony in the melt, and in 18th-century Europe it was to rival porcelain in translucency and strength. Opalescent glass, perfected in the United States toward the end of the 19th century, has a milky opaque appearance, with colours streaked through it.

Modern Glass and Methods

The invention in England of the float-glass process in the 1950s has now made all other methods of producing clear flat glass obsolete.

In this technique the liquid glass is floated on a bed of molten tin, producing almost perfectly smooth parallel sides to give great clarity – and allow cheap mass-production.

New techniques in decorative drawn or rolled glass include coating its surface with hot glue to produce surface fractures, adding small particles or chips of different colours to the cooling surface in manufacture, and creating by other methods ever more varied surface effects, such as the increasingly popular American ripped "water" glass. Fusing one glass with another is a growing area of interest, and can allow many contrasting colours in a single piece of glass. More and more, it seems the only limitation of the type of glass that can be produced is the glassmaker's imagination.

NEW PRODUCTION METHODS

As flat glass became more widely used for general window glazing, so new methods of production were invented to meet the growing demand. Two methods revolutionized glassmaking at the beginning of the 19th century – the first, drawing a ribbon of glass vertically from the melt, letting it cool as it travelled away from the furnace and then cutting it up into sheets, and, second, rolling glass by passing it in a treacly state through two rollers to flatten it into a ribbon. The later refinement of polishing the surface of the glass produced the smooth clarity of plate glass. Rolling and drawing also provided the means of making a cheap and plentiful supply of coloured glass to meet the growing demand for stained glass. Referred to as "cathedral" glass, it lacks the character and beauty of "antique" glass; when a second colour is included, it is known as "streaky cathedral." The use of rollers also allowed pattern

LEFT AND OPPOSITE PAGE *Glass-blowers' tools.*

and texture to be pressed onto the glass in its manufacture and, although most commonly found in clear glass, patterned coloured glass is also made – sometimes to try and imitate the striations on the surface of "antique" glass.

In the 19th century, box-shaped molds were introduced in which molten glass was blown against the sides, and, when solidified, cut up into rectangles. These slabs of glass were thick in the centre and tapered to a

thinner edge, giving great depth of colour and beauty. It was developed in 1889 by E.S. Prior and, because of its resemblance to 13th-century glass, it was known as Prior's Early English. Chance Brothers made a similar glass that they called Norman.

Health and Safety

Stained glass is a fun and rewarding pastime, but it is crucial that proper health and safety precautions are followed in order to protect yourself and those who will come into contact with the materials and equipment you use.

Stained glass artistry can be a safe, rewarding hobby if the proper steps are taken in the studio. Many of the safety issues are typical of the workshop, such as wearing safety goggles when cutting or grinding.

However, in stained glass work the lead safety issue is paramount. Because lead is toxic, it requires special precautions to protect the health of stained glass artists and their families as well as the environment. And while the hazardous nature of lead may sound intimidating, simple blood tests can provide peace of mind as to the effectiveness of one's lead handling safety practices.

Although there are alternatives, lead remains the favoured choice of many stained glass artists for joining pieces of glass due to its malleability and resistance to corrosion. For these reasons, professional studios continue to use lead came. Before you do so, it is worth getting seeking advice. Hobbyists in Britain can refer to the Health and Safety Executive, who will be able to provide you with information on lead use in the home. Similarly, you can contact your local environmental health officer for advice.

Hobbyists who prefer not to deal with lead issues may opt to join glass pieces with copper foil or lead-free came and to create pieces that do not utilize lead paints. Once you have looked at the health issues, you may decide that this is the right course of action for you. But for the rest of us, a brief lead education is in order.

Lead has been identified as a toxin that accumulates in the human body, creating a hazard to human health as well as a hazardous waste product. Lead's primary routes into the body are through inhalation and ingestion, so certain safety practices are directed at preventing these. It is worth noting that studies have shown inhalation to produce up to ten times the poisonous effects of ingestion and that glass painting with paints containing lead produces the greatest health risk.

The hazards of lead exposure will enter the home if proper precautions are not taken by stained glass artists who choose to use lead came.

Children and pets are the most susceptible to lead intoxication, which can cause learning disabilities and even death. For this reason, women who are pregnant or planning to conceive must not work with lead. Lead exposure greatly increases the risk of miscarriage, stillbirth and birth defects.

TOP 20 SAFETY PRECAUTIONS FOR THE HOME STUDIO

This list of essential safety measures is brief, but may serve as an introduction:

1. Limit activities to what you can safely accommodate. Making small windows joined with copperfoil or lead-free cames and not painting on glass would be the safest. Lead-free solder is available.

2. Keep those most susceptible to the harmful effects of lead poisoning – pregnant women, children and pets – outside the work area.

3. Do not eat, drink or smoke in the work area because lead dust can be easily ingested or inhaled.

4. Establish a well-ventilated work area that is separated from your living space. Take care that your workspace does not contain air returns that might contaminate the home ventilation system.

5. The studio must be separate or at least closed off from the rest of the living space. Adhesive walk mats in the doorways may assist in collecting lead. Separate shoes should be worn in the studio and the home.

6. Provide separate hand-washing facilities and a telephone in the studio. Artists must not enter the home in work clothes to wash up or answer the phone.

7. Do not sweep or dust the workspace. Obtain a high efficiency particulate air (HEPA) vacuum and use it for cleanup. Take time to properly change the filters and properly dispose of them.

8. Choose non-porous work surfaces and flooring and wet-mop them regularly with tri-sodium phosphate (TSP) or another lead-cleansing cleaner.

9. Store scrap lead to be recycled in containers that have tight-fitting lids and provide sealed storage for paints.

10. Existing windows should not be de-leaded in the home studio. Lead oxides found in older cames are extremely toxic and must be handled accordingly. Restoration is a job for the professional studio.

11. Wear protective clothing such as

coveralls and gloves to keep lead dust from settling on the body and skin. Change clothing and shoes before leaving the work area to prevent the tracking of lead. Wash these clothes separately from other laundry.

12. Wear safety glasses to protect your eyes.

13. Wear a double cartridge high efficiency particulate air (HEPA) respirator when soldering or working in any operation that produces dust or fumes, including glass painting or panel dismantling. Respirators should be professionally specified and personally fitted, and the filter should be effective to .3 microns or as specified.

14. Always wash your hands, ideally with a soap formulated for metal removal before eating, drinking or smoking after lead exposure.

15. After working with lead, you may want to HEPA vacuum lead from your clothing and hair. Ideally, shower in a facility separate from the home to rid the body and hair of lead dust.

16. Monitor your blood lead with regular blood tests.

17. Contact the Health and Safety Executive and your local environmental officer for advice.

18. Properly use and store equipment and hazardous substances. Read and follow manufacturer's instructions and/or material data safety sheets.

19. Try the new lead-free came, which you may be able to find from British suppliers.

20. Dispose of lead waste safely. Many suppliers provide recycling. Contact your local council and/or your local environmental health officer for advice.

SAFETY BASICS

EMERGENCY PREPAREDNESS
It is important to keep current with safety issues, post emergency contact numbers, maintain first aid supplies, including an eyewash station and have a working fire extinguisher available.

FLAMMABLES
Flammables must be properly labelled and must be stored in a flammable materials cabinet away from heat or spark sources.

KNOWLEDGE OF PRODUCTS AND EQUIPMENT
Carefully read and follow the instructions for proper use of all products and equipment. Protection for the eyes, face, hearing and respiration will likely be needed for various tasks. If

hobbyists elect to install a kiln, proper installation and use are essential.

PROPER USE OF RESPIRATORS

For protection against lead exposure and other air contaminants, cartridges approved for that particular type and level of protection must be used. Respirators must be properly stored and maintained.

GLASS HANDLING AND STORAGE

Care must be taken in the storage and handling of glass to minimize the chance of being hurt. Taking the following precautions will help avoid injury.

✳ Never store glass above head height.

✳ Storage racks should be designed for vertical glass storage and be adequately secured and strong enough to bear the glass load.

✳ Minimize glass handling by locating glass storage areas conveniently to workstations.

✳ Ensure that the worktable is clean and free of tools before moving glass.

✳ Check floor for slipping or tripping hazards before carrying glass.

✳ Wearing gloves, goggles, long-sleeved coveralls, and reinforced shoes or boots will provide added protection.

✳ Prior to picking up a sheet of glass, check it for cracks. Look it over first, then test for invisible cracks by tapping it with your knuckle. A healthy sheet will have a singular, clear ring, while a cracked sheet will have a multiple, off-key resound.

✳ Always carry glass in a vertical position. A sheet of glass should be picked up and carried by grasping it with both hands along the top edge. However, for heavier sheets, one hand on the top edge and one supporting the bottom edge or side may be necessary.

✳ Do not slide your hand along the edge of a piece of glass, even with gloves on.

✳ Carefully watch clearance between the edge of the table and the glass you are carrying.

✳ To safely place a sheet of glass on your work table, continue to hold it with one hand on the top. Move the other to the bottom edge and rest the center of the glass against the edge of the table vertically, then tilt up horizontally and ease the glass onto the table.

✳ Work tables should be large enough to avoid having glass hang over the edges.

✳ Prior to putting cut-offs in scrap bins,

it is a good idea to remove acute points for safer retrieval. Scrap glass should be placed, not tossed, into its bin.

SAFETY IN SPECIFIC TASKS

Note: It is advisable to wear a double cartridge HEPA respirator when soldering or working in any operation that produces dust or dust fumes, including glass painting or dismantling. Refer to manufacturer's instruction, as other types of respirators such as supplied air may be required based on air monitoring results.

✱ Glass cutting: Follow manufacturer's instructions for equipment use. With a traditional hand glass cutter, safety glasses should be worn and the worktable surface should be HEPA vacuumed of any scrap glass. Extra care should be taken in handling and cutting textured glass.

✱ Glass grinding: Follow manufacturer's instructions for use. Have a face shield affixed to the grinder to protect the face and eyes. The grinder should be equipped with local exhaust due to the millions of particles of powdered glass that are hazardous themselves and also may contain arsenic, cadmium, selenium, and other colorants. Always keep water in the grinder as required by the instructions, but do not allow the grinder to sit in water, as it is an electrical appliance. Users must wear safety goggles.

✱ Glass painting: Vitreous paints contain hazardous materials, usually metal compounds. They typically contain large amounts of lead and an exposure over the safe particulate limit, thus requiring an exhaust system or respirators.

✱ Glazing: In fitting lead came, caution must be taken in cutting, fitting and in brushing. Gloves should be worn to protect the skin. If an electric saw or brush is used, this may require use of a respirator or local exhaust system.

✱ Firing: Thermal gloves should be worn when handling hot glass. Special protective goggles are available to resist the heat. Wear natural fibre or flame retardant clothing, which is less hazardous in case of fire. If a kiln has been installed, it must be properly vented due to hazardous emissions. Follow all manufacturers' instructions.

✱ Soldering/Fluxing: Follow manufacturer's instructions for use because most fluxes contain toxic materials such as zinc chloride. Flux and soldering fumes should be vented or respirators should be worn. Zinc chloride also harms the eyes and skin, so eye protection is advisable as are long sleeves and cotton gloves if you will touch the piece. Do not touch the eyes or skin with flux or solder on your hands. Wash hands after use.

✳ Cementing: A respirator should be worn while cementing, as well as eye protection due to the use of whiting (calcium carbonate). Panels should be cleaned with a HEPA vacuum, and an exhaust fan with a HEPA filter is also advisable. Latex or rubber gloves are recommended.

✳ Applying patina: Again, it is important to read manufacturer's instructions. Patina should not be used with steel wool, which can create a chemical reaction and burn. Rubber gloves and an apron should be worn when applying patina. Both copper and black patinas contain chemicals that will dissolve sponges and clothing. Wear proper protective clothing.

SANDBLASTING SAFETY (FOR ETCHING)

Sandblasting presents unique safety challenges and may best be contracted to specialists. Due to the high velocity at which the sand is propelled for etching, millions of tiny silica particles are released into the air in the process. It is most important that the lungs be protected from silica dust, which can cause chronic respiratory disease or even death.

The safety equipment needed will vary depending on whether etching is done in a self-contained blasting cabinet or not. In any case, follow the manufacturer's instructions for your materials. Use proper respiratory protection, eye protection and protective clothing.

If the noise from the machinery is loud, or when blasting at higher pressures, it is advisable to wear ear plugs or other hearing protectors.

THE DANGERS OF HYDROFLUORIC ACID

Hydrofluoric acid is used by professionals for removing flash in flash glass or other types of etching. This acid is extremely dangerous and should not be used by the hobbyist. Safe handling of hydrofluoric acid requires specialized training and equipment to prevent catastrophic injury (due to latency, severe burn damage can occur without being immediately painful or apparent) or death. Hydrofluoric acid should never be used in the home studio and cannot be safely stored in the home.

ENVIRONMENTAL PROTECTION

Metallic lead should be recycled. It is also essential to safely contain and dispose of lead waste and wastewater, if produced. You can contact your local council for information regarding disposal requirements for toxic substances used in the studio.

Every craft has its safety issues, and thankfully, with stained glass, today the issues are known and can be properly addressed. When these are followed, stained glass artistry can be a safe, rewarding hobby.

Disclaimer: THESE RECOMMENDATIONS ARE NOT A SUBSTITUTE FOR REGULATORY SAFETY STANDARDS. Contact the Health and Safety Executive (HSE) or your local environmental health officer for advice.

RESOURCES FOR SAFETY ISSUES

The Health and Safety Executive (HSE)
(1G) Redgrave Court
Merton Road
Bootle
Merseyside, L20 7HS
0845 345 0055
www.hse.gov.uk

Chartered Institute of Environmental Health (CIEH)
Chadwick Court
15 Hatfields
London, SE1 8DJ
020 7928 6006
www.cieh.org
Organisation set up to promote environmental health.

You should also contact your local council for advice, and they will be able to put you in touch with your local environmental health officer.

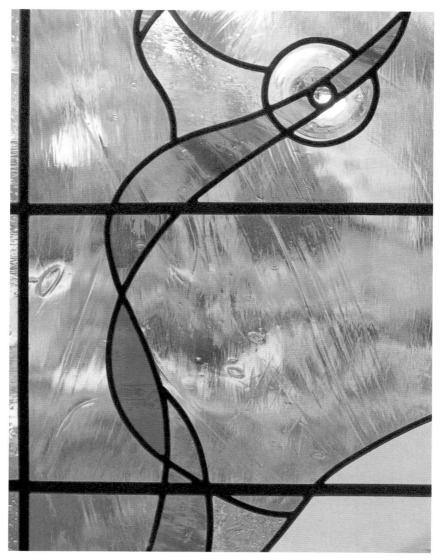

As long as health and safety precautions are followed, you will be free to create beautiful designs like this without posing danger to yourself or your family.

Glass

It's hard to imagine a world without the
plain, featureless material known as glass.
From fibre optics used in communications
to an everyday wine bottle, glass is a
material that has woven itself into every
corner of our daily lives. Aside from new,
efficient manufacturing processes, the actual
make-up of glass has remained basically
unchanged from the first crude vessel cast
in the ancient world.

Which Glass to Choose?

'How well does it cut?' is very often the first question we are asked and unfortunately, there is no firm answer.

Today, there is a vast range of coloured and clear glass from which to choose, both hand- and machine-made. The principal ingredients to all types of glass are silica sand, soda ash and limestone. The soda ash acts as a flux facilitating the melting sand, while the limestone is added as a stabilizer, making the finished product more durable. Colours in glass are created by blending natural metallic oxides into the raw materials. Cadmium sulphide creates yellow, cobalt creates blue, while true pinks can be made only with gold.

ABOVE *Red flashed glass reveals a traditional floral pattern.*
BELOW *A starburst design on brilliant blue flashed glass.*

Glass manufacturing has been – and still is – very much a process of experimenting, adjusting and personalising the basic recipe to achieve a variety of results. Glass artists today benefit from a huge range of glass supplied by different manufacturers, each offering his own individual and identifiable product.

Buying glass for your project is a stimulating process; it's satisfying to assess the many colours and textures while trying to visualise how they can be worked into your design.

Glass is divided into two general types: antique or mouth blown glass and machine-made glass. Within these two groups are many sub-groups of specialised glass.

After glass has been formed into sheets it is slowly heated and then cooled. This process – called annealing – removes the stress or tension within the sheet, making it possible to cut. Glass that hasn't been well annealed is termed "fiery", often breaking erratically when scored with the cutter. Antique glass occasionally has this tendency, more so when making the first cut on a full stock sheet. Hot colours such as red and yellow can also be slightly more difficult to cut as the glass itself has a harder surface.

ANTIQUE GLASS

Favoured by glass artists, each sheet of antique glass is blown into a cylinder or "muff", which is annealed, cut down the length with a glass cutter, and reheated to be flattened into a sheet. The individual skills and years of experience required to become a proficient glass-maker necessitate that antique glass is more expensive than machine-made glass. The uneven texture, brilliant surface qualities and array of "imperfections" give each sheet a distinctive character.

PLAIN ANTIQUE: Only one colour.

STREAKY ANTIQUE: Two or more colours swirled together, making sheets of this glass appear like a delicate watercolour painting locked within each sheet.

CLEAR REAMY: Available in clear or tint colours. Each sheet is characterised by great surface movement giving the glass a "windy" effect.

SEEDY AND CLEAR: Light tints or clear glass that has been purposely made with the air bubbles to distort and refract light.

CRACKLE: Antique glass that is rapidly cooled to distress the surface.

FLASHED: A thin layer or flash of glass laid on a base colour or clear glass. The thin flash can then be etched or sandblasted away, exposing the contrasting base colour.

SEMI-ANTIQUE GLASS

Midway between blown antique and machine-rolled glass is semi-antique. Often called drawn antique, this type of glass is pulled or drawn from the molten furnace and allowed to anneal and harden in air, giving it a smooth and brilliant surface on both sides. Available in many colour tints, with either a plain or wavy surface, semi-antique is considerably less expensive than the handmade variety.

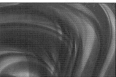

LEFT *It's tremendously exciting to see the enormous range of coloured glass now available. These examples of streaky antique glass demonstrate the wonderful array of colours and patterns you can buy for your projects.*

MACHINE-ROLLED GLASS

Nowhere has the interest in art glass become more apparent than in the manufacture of rolled colour glass. Glass manufacturers both in the United States and Europe offer hundreds of colours, patterns and densities. As the name implies, the molten glass is rolled out by machine on a flat surface. Various textures and patterns can be impressed on the semi-fluid glass surface as it is passed through rollers. Like antique glass, the various rolled glass manufacturers each have their own particular style of creating glass that is easily identifiable. Because of its lower cost, availability, and diversity, rolled glass is the most frequently used glass for newcomers.

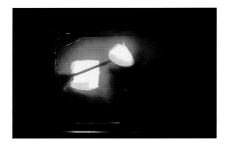

The primary glass furnace with 30 tons of hot glass. To this is added the particular colour being produced. This method of production known as "continuous ribbon" is unique to Spectrum.

Examples of Machine-rolled glass

The actual production of rolled glass is an exciting feast of colour, heat and motion. Glass manufacturers, Spectrum have combined modern technology with Old World methods to produce an extensive range of quality machine glass.

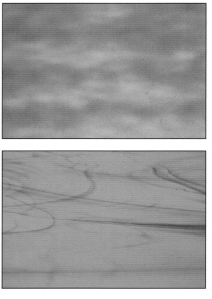

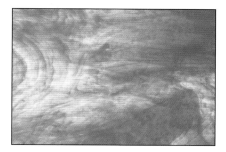

OPPOSITE PAGE AND LEFT *Less expensive than hand-fabricated glass, machine-rolled glass is nevertheless produced in a wide range of types, styles and colours.*

HAND-ROLLED GLASS

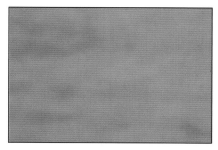

Each piece of special art glass is individually hand rolled creating details, colours and textures that could never be duplicated by machine. Glass similar to the innovative work of Tiffany continues to be produced by small specialized companies concentrating on this beautiful and unusual glass.

Glass types

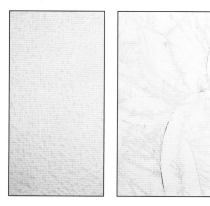

ABOVE AND FOLLOWING PAGE *A selection of hand-rolled glass; no two sheets will be identical.*

 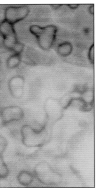 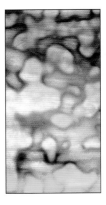 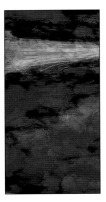

Fracture and streamer glass

The production of fracture and streamer glass by the Uroboros Glass Company. First, a large bubble is blown then broken; that creates the fractures. The molten fractures and streamers are spread by hand as the sheet is rolled out.

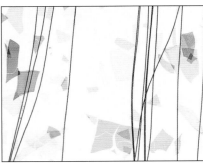

ROUNDELS AND NUGGETS

Roundels and nuggets are wonderfully tactile small pieces of glass used for various decorative purposes. Nuggets, for example, are often used in projects other than stained glasswork, jewellery being one. Roundels are beautiful pieces of glass that the manufacturer makes by spinning molten glass into small circles. These are available in a wide range of colours for use in Victorian-style leaded lights.

CUT GLASS GEMS

Cut glass gems are rather like nuggets, but instead they are made with many facets and highly polished to reflect the light. Gems radiate colour and, in some cases, will refract light.

Examples of roundels and nuggets

Circles of coloured glass with smooth edges come in various sizes. They are either hand spun or pressed by machine and used most frequently in leaded lights.

Cut glass gems

Examples of Baroque glass

RIGHT
These two pieces of Baroque glass on the right are iridized.

Examples of plain antique/antique streaky

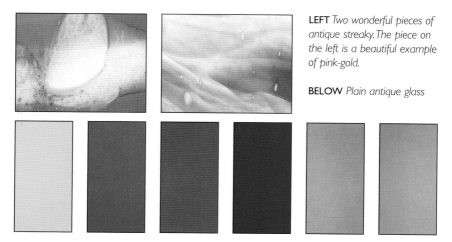

LEFT *Two wonderful pieces of antique streaky. The piece on the left is a beautiful example of pink-gold.*

BELOW *Plain antique glass*

How to Work with Glass

Not surprisingly, many beginners are nervous when handling glass, frightened it might break easily and that they could injure themselves. Although glass is fragile, it is also remarkably robust. How you handle it is often the key to success. This chapter focuses on the basic skills of glass cutting; the tools you will need, and the techniques to develop. Once you gain confidence, cutting and handling glass will, like most skills, become second nature.

Working With Glass

Like any other craft or trade, stained glass has its own specialized range of tools and materials. The tools of the trade are, in fact, perfect examples of logic and simplicity.

Glasswork is very much a hands-on craft and the tools have evolved to fit the hand comfortably for a specific function. Much of the equipment that has been introduced in the last 20 years is in response to the growing demand from hobbyists for easier and more convenient tools. With relatively little outlay, an individual can purchase a basic set of tools enabling him or her to create intricate, professional results — remember, the skill is in the hand, not the tool!

Because stained glass is a specialized craft, we recommend the best place to start looking for information is with a specialized company. A general tool merchant or glass shop is generally not able to advise or supply you so well. There are many small glass studios that both create their own work and offer a supply service. Look in the telephone book under "Stained Glass" and find out if they have a genuine interest in the supply of tools and information. A good supplier will be invaluable, not only for the basics but also for advice on techniques and materials as your work progresses. Very often, a catalogue will be available providing both a mail order service and a helpful description of products.

CUTTING EQUIPMENT

GLASS CUTTERS

A glass cutter is not actually a cutter in the traditional sense like a hacksaw or scissors. In fact, glass isn't really cut in any way that resembles the cutting of wood, metal or cloth. The glass cutter offers a much more subtle method of changing large pieces of glass into smaller, intricate shapes. All glass cutters have a hard steel wheel that will scratch or score the glass surface. We always recommend that you purchase the best cutter you can afford as this tool is really the key to working with glass. Although the quality of the cutters will vary from a cheap plastic handle cutter through a sophisticated charmer with a brass handle and oil reservoir, it is really the skill and technique of the individual that is most important. To date, there are literally dozens of different cutters on the market made to fit the hand comfortably. Like feet, hands are quite particular to the individual and it's best to "try on" several styles to discover the one that feels right before making a purchase. When considering different types of glass cutter, don't choose a multiple wheel cutter. These are generally of a poor quality and even worse, the large head will hide the cut line from view, which is in effect like driving with a blindfold. Diamond cutters, tricky to use, are only suitable for straight lines and should not be considered for use in stained glass.

The most important part of any cutter is the cutting wheel. The quality of the wheel will influence how well and how long the cutter will last. We can divide glass cutters into three general groups by the type of wheel.

LEFT *Ball end cutter with tungsten carbide steel wheel.*

RIGHT *Cutter with an oil resevoir.*

Steel wheel cutter: The classic pencil grip cutter with or without a ball end has been cutting glass since the mid-1800s. Most people will be introduced to cutting with this tool and although it looks painfully simple when compared to newer shapes, it is a precise and capable tool. The three grooves or indentations on this cutter were at one time covered with a soft metal and used to shape glass. The soft metal insertions are no longer available, making the grooves on the classic cutter about as useful as tailfins on a car. The steel wheel cutter is a good introductory tool, but it will soon wear out.

Carbide steel cutters: Although identical in appearance to steel, these offer at least five times more life and require less pressure, making them easier to use. When making the transition from steel to carbide steel, most people will initially apply excessive pressure and score the glass too deeply. The ball end cutter illustrated is available with a replaceable carbide wheel and is the favoured tool of many older glass cutters who learned on this venerable classic. It has a cast iron handle, a weighty feel, and is a pleasure to use.

Tungsten carbide steel: The third general type of cutters were introduced to the market relatively recently and if the term "revolutionise glass cutting" can be applied, these cutters would get the credit. The cutting wheel is upgraded to tungsten carbide steel and is much smaller in diameter than the conventional carbide or steel wheel. Smaller, harder wheels translate into less pressure and are therefore easier to control when scoring. Like turning on a bike with small tires,

LEFT AND FAR LEFT
Cutters with oil resevoirs.

these cutters are excellent for intricate pieces with the tight curves favoured by many glassworkers today.

Designers of these cutters have also applied the science of ergonomics by creating handles that fit the hand with a natural, easy grip. These tools, known as the super cutters, have introduced glass cutting to many people who never felt at ease with the pencil shape of the classic. Most will contain an oil reservoir that constantly lubricates the cutting wheel when scoring. Some can be gripped like a tennis racket; others have thick handles large enough to accommodate two hands when cutting.

Glass cutters, like toothbrushes, are very personal items and shouldn't be loaned or borrowed. If properly cared for they can give years of good service, however, the cutting wheel will eventually wear out and need to be replaced. There are companies that will resharpen dull cutting wheels but usually

RIGHT
Lubricate your cutter from time to time with cutting oil. It will keep the glass cutter clean and well oiled. Keep a jar by your work area with a pad of cotton dampened in kerosene or a lightweight cutting oil available from stained glass suppliers. Lubricating the wheel will prolong its life and improve the score on the surface of the glass. Some glass cutters have a reservoir or chamber that can be filled with cutting oil.

the expense and time involved makes replacement a better alternative.

GLASS PLIERS

Second only to the glass cutter, glass pliers are the tool you will become most familiar with when working glass. Pliers are used for shaping and breaking glass after it has been scored with the cutter. Although similar in appearance to a pair of general household pliers, glass pliers are very specialized and are easily damaged if used for repairing your bicycle, or mending your fence. In studio work most people tend to use three types of pliers in their

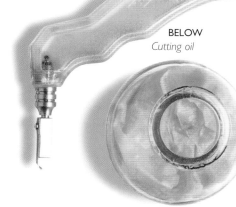

RIGHT
Pistol-grip cutter

BELOW
Cutting oil

day-to-day work. Pliers made for the glazing trade are heavy-handed tools for working with plate glass and are seldom used with coloured glasswork.

Grozier pliers: The grozier pliers are by far the most important pliers in your tool box and are in constant use for a great many tasks. Made from a soft metal, the lower jaw of the pliers is curved and serrated to grip and hold the glass effectively. Most groziers are now supplied with a spring-loaded handle that returns to the open position when in use, thus reducing fatigue. The primary use of the grozier is to nibble and shape irregular pieces of glass; its narrow jaw width makes the grozier particularly suitable for reaching inside curves.

Breaking pliers: Breaking pliers tend to get the most use when someone has either borrowed or misplaced the grozier. Usually slightly heavier than a grozier, with wider jaws, the breakers are used for breaking off straight-line scores on larger sections of glass.

Running pliers: Long, straight and narrow pieces of glass will often break in two (or three) when separated from a larger sheet. The running pliers are constructed solely for the purpose of successfully separating these thin, sometimes difficult, straight cuts. The inside of the jaws are either curved or have a raised centre section that is lined up directly over a cut. When pressure is applied to the score it will very often run with a satisfying click, neatly separating a thin strip of glass. Available in plastic or metal, the running pliers are a useful tool for their very specific task.

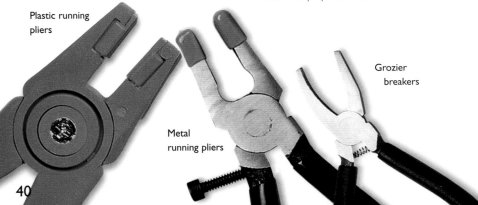

Snippers

Plastic running pliers

Metal running pliers

Grozier breakers

GRINDING

Electric glass grinder

When running beginners' workshops, most teacher choose to keep this machine well hidden under the table. So strong is the allure of the grinder that, given the chance, many students would learn glass grinding rather than glass cutting. Glass pushed against the water-cooled, diamond-impregnated, spinning wheel becomes perfectly smooth with minimal effort. The shape of a piece of glass can be changed in seconds. Beginners will often rely too much on the machine rather than perfecting their skills of accurate cutting. Once you are confident with a cutter and pliers, however, the grinder becomes a valuable, labour-saving machine that will encourage you to move on to more ambitious projects.

Various bit sizes and grits can be installed that will either aggressively remove an area of glass or leave an almost polished edge. Care must be taken to keep the water coolant level high and always to wear eye protection if the machine is not fitted with an eye shield.

Carborundum or whetstone

As many of us painfully know, glass frequently breaks with a razor sharp edge. The carborundum stone dulls the edges, making them safe to handle. Although time consuming, compared with the electric grinding machine, the carborundum stone is inexpensive and effective. You can whet the stone to minimize glass dust, and to use, simply rub the edges of the glass along the sides of the stone.

Electric grinding machine and safety goggles.

41

USEFUL AIDS FOR GLASS CUTTING

Most glass cutting is freehand, so it's just you, your cutter and the glass. Stained glass windows for the most part are one-of-a-kind designs that usually do not require a great many repetitive, identical shapes. However, cutting aids exist that make short, accurate work of tasks that could otherwise take hours by freehand with less than perfect results.

THE CUTTING SQUARE

No matter how steady your hand, the only way to cut a perfectly straight line is to use a cutting edge or square. The squares that are used for glass cutting have a 90 degree runner or stop along the lower edge that both prevents the

edge from moving and gives a perfect square cut. This is especially useful for squaring off sheets when it is necessary to work from a straight line. Squares are available in many lengths and most studios will require a long one – around 90 cm (one yard) – for cutting down stock sheets and several smaller ones for squaring up individual pieces.

THE CIRCLE-STRIP CUTTER

Learning to cut a circle freehand is an important skill that encompasses many vital cutting steps. However, like a straight line, a perfectly round circle can be cut only with a specific circle cutter. Circles are not a frequent shape in glass design but the circle cutter has a certain novelty value that some people will find hard to resist. A turret with

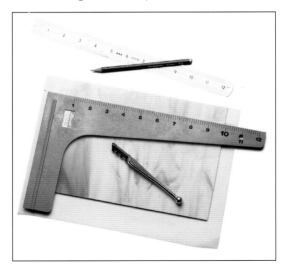

either a suction cup or rubber tip legs is held firmly on the glass surface. A metal rod with an adjustable cutting head rotates around the axis of this turret scoring the glass. Beam cutters of this type will cut circles as small as 7.6 cm (3 inches) in diameter.

The strip cutter is usually supplied with the circle cutter and is used to cut long, straight strips. The turret used on the circle cutter is substituted for a guide that follows along the

straight edge of a sheet. The length of
strip is simply determined by the size
of the sheet.

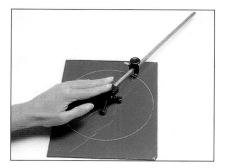

The rubber feet grip the centre of the glass
and the cutting head is positioned on the
guideline.

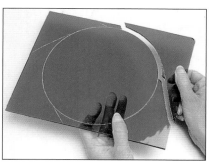

Once the glass has been scored, tangent scores
must be made so the circle can be broken
easily.

IRREGULAR SHAPE CUTTER

Few glass artists would require this
type of machine for bulk cutting or
repetitious shapes. Shape cutters are
generally used in production studios
where quantities of perfect repeats are
required for lampshades or
lightcatchers. A glass cutting wheel,
mounted on a stylus is guided around a
template, making an identical score on
each piece of glass. The pressure of the
score on the glass is regulated by
compressed air, making these machines
incredibly fast and simple to use.

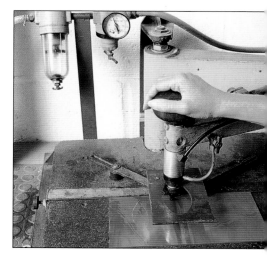

Glass Cutting

Cutting glass is not as difficult as many people imagine. By following some simple but essential guidelines you will soon develop confidence in your glass-cutting abilities.

Persevere and practise on clear scrap glass. There are several recommended ways of holding a cutter, but there are now several types of cutter on the market and styles of holding the cutter for comfort and efficiency will vary. Here, one of the most popular styles has been emphasised because most students find that it works best.

However, individual preference will develop and, providing the chosen method produces the desired result without unnecessary effort, there's no reason why you shouldn't use it.

Ask a glass merchant to let you have some offcuts of thin clear window glass, which is easy to work with and cheap for practising.

IMPORTANT HINTS

* Always stand when cutting glass and work on a flat and steady work surface.
* Make sure your table is not too high; just below waist level is recommended.
* Never go over the score in a different place on the glass. Going over the old score again will just create a dull gouge in the glass and in time will ruin the cutting wheel.
* If the glass is textured, always score on the smooth side.
* If you do not hear the sound of scoring on the glass, then it is more than likely that you are not using enough pressure.
* Do not lift the cutter off the glass until the score is complete.
* Always make sure that a score travels from one edge of the glass to another. You cannot start or stop in the middle of a piece of glass.
* Keep a dustpan and brush next to you and remember to make a habit of brushing up the shards of glass as you work.

HOW TO HOLD THE CUTTER

1. *There are several ways to hold a cutter. The traditional way is to position the cutter between the forefinger and middle finger and hold the thumb on the inside curve of the cutter. However, if you find this uncomfortable, try gripping the cutter firmly between the index finger and thumb with the index finger on top. Allow the shank to rest in the hollow of your hand.*

2. *Sometimes it helps to use the other hand for extra pressure. Place the thumb of the other hand on the end of the cutter and stretch the fingers down to rest pressure next to the cutting head.*

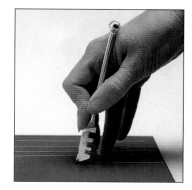

3. *Place the cutter on the glass at about an angle of just below 90 degrees. Practise scoring by placing the cutting wheel at the near edge of the glass and press the cutter down while pushing slowly and steadily to the other edge of the glass. You should bear down with enough pressure to be able to hear the wheel scoring the surface. Keep the pressure and the speed constant. The score will appear as a fracture on the glass.*

WORK SURFACE

A hard wood or similar tabletop will cause the glass to slide around and become scratched, so it must be covered. Many people use cardboard, cork, heavy craft paper, a thin pile or carpet underlay with good results. Keep a pan and brush handy and frequently brush off the tiny shards of glass that will be produced on every cut. You are more likely to obtain small cuts with these tiny needles of glass when you inadvertently brush them off the table with your hand than at any other time. Use a brush!

Experiment by adjusting the positions of your finger and thumb slightly and by changing the angle at which you hold the cutter to give a better score. If your score is too faint, apply more pressure until you can both see and hear the cut line appear. How you feel most comfortable holding the cutter will vary according to the style of cutter. How well you have scored the glass will become evident when you begin to break the score apart. Scored glass should always be broken or snapped while the score is still new.

To break the piece of glass apart once it has been scored, you can use one of several methods shown opposite and overleaf.

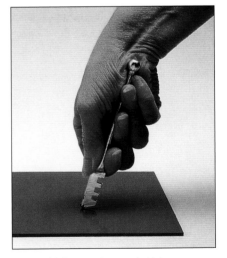

ABOVE *Make sure that you hold the cutter comfortably. Adjust your fingers and thumb and the angle of the cutter until you feel relaxed.*

Hands

Achieving a clean break is one of the most satisfying aspects of cutting, and you will feel a great sense of achievement when you break a score using just your hands.

Hold the scored piece firmly, with a thumb on each side of the score line and with your index fingers underneath and either side of the score; snap the glass by moving your wrists sharply outward. Always keep your thumbs and fingers next to the score and grip the glass firmly while snapping apart.

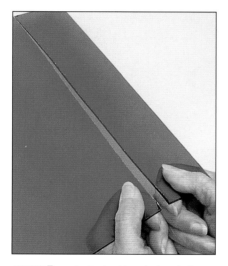

ABOVE *To snap apart a piece by hand, place the thumbs on top and curl the fingers underneath and either side of the score. Make a sharp outward movement of the wrist while gripping the glass between the fingers and thumb.*

Glass pliers

Pliers are especially useful when you want to break off a piece of glass that is too small or very narrow or just awkward to be broken by hand. Place the tip of the pliers next to the score line. Hold the glass tightly in one hand and grip the glass well with the pliers in the other. While gripping the glass with the pliers, pull and snap apart.

Glass pliers are also used to break off any small irregular edges on a straight or curved score.

ABOVE *If the strip of glass you want is too narrow for your fingers, use the pliers. Put the edge of the pliers in line with the score and grip the glass. Keep the fingers and thumbs of the other hand close to the score and hold the glass steady.*

BELOW *Glass does not always break just as you would like. Trim the score with the pliers. Always place the pliers next to the score and with a firm and confident grip, snap off the unwanted glass.*

TAPPING

Tapping is particularly useful and often necessary for breaking curved scores and is the most reliable method of encouraging a score to break on difficult glass. If you feel you have made a good score but are unable to break the glass apart with your hands or the pliers, tapping will usually help you out. As you tap you will see the appearance of the score change as a fracture develops.

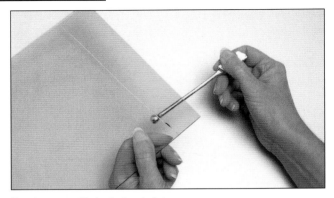

Tap the score with the ball end of the cutter.

To break the glass, hold the cutter with your fingers and thumb

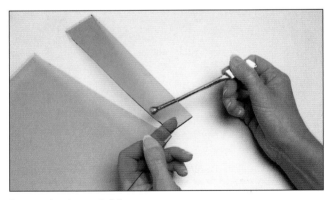

Support the glass as it falls apart.

and tap directly on the score line from underneath with the ball end of the cutter. As you tap, the appearance of the line should begin to change. If it does not, tap a little harder, still taking care to strike the glass directly under the score line. Hold the piece of glass very firmly while you tap, supporting it in preparation for pieces falling on the table. When tapping remember that you need only give a controlled but very firm "tap" under the score. There is no need to swing the ball cutter wildly.

BENCH METHOD

You can break a larger piece of glass in two by placing the scored lines on the edge of a table, then raise the glass and bring it back down again sharply. The downward force will cause the score to break on the edge of the table. This procedure can be used only for straight cuts. Don't use this method on anything larger than one square foot of glass.

After you have scored and broken some pieces of glass you will notice there may be tiny protrusions and sometimes narrow slices of glass on the edges of the glass. These can be taken off using the same pliers you used for breaking. This is called grozing. By holding the glass gently between the jaws of the pliers and rolling the pliers up or down, you will be able to remove these small slivers. A tiny chip on the edge of the glass that refuses to shift can be all that prevents your piece of glass from fitting perfectly. Take it off by squeezing the chip with the tip of the pliers and literally nipping it away with a sharp downward movement of the pliers.

Use the edge of the table to help break the glass.

Untidy edges can be grozed off. Close the pliers over the glass. Maintain a loose hold and rotate them gently up or down. The "teeth" inside the mouth of the pliers will groze away these edges.

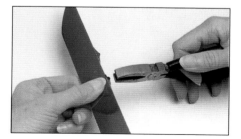

Small jagged bits of glass can be "nipped" away. Use just the tip of the pliers to hold the glass, squeeze them, and nip off the tiny pieces.

CUTTING A WAVY LINE

After practising scoring and breaking random lines across some scrap glass, try some wavy lines or actual shapes. Practise breaking with your hands and also the pliers. Right angles cannot be cut from glass and to cut certain shapes there are particular rules to follow.

1. *Simple carved shapes can usually be broken with pliers but occasionally – depending on the type of glass – there may be some resistance. A few short, sharp taps with the ball end of the cutter can help to release the tension in the score. As you tap, you will see the score change in appearance.*

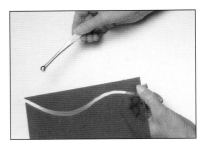

2. *Support the glass while you tap.*

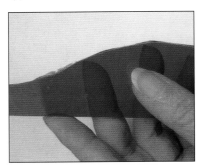

3. *Once the curve has been tapped it will probably still show jagged edges. These must be grozed away.*

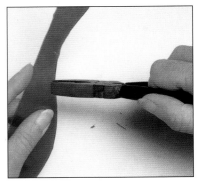

4. *Groze the edges using the pliers. Hold the pliers gently, don't grip too tightly, and rotate them. The "teeth" of the pliers will remove these pieces.*

CUTTING ANGLES

You cannot simply cut a right or acute angle from a piece of glass. Instead, you must plan your scores carefully to enable you to achieve the desired result. Below, we show how to cut a right angle and a "v" shape in glass.

1. The dotted lines indicate the necessary direction of the scores, the first one being the vertical.

2. The first score is broken.

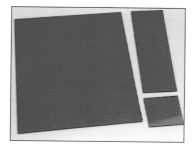

3. The second score is broken.

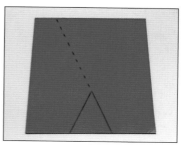

4. The "v" could not be cut out of a piece of glass by hand unless you follow the dotted lines that indicate the first score.

CUTTING A CIRCLE

True circles must be scored first with a circle cutter (see pages 42-43). Once this is done, you will need to make many tangent scores of the circle for the glass to break correctly.

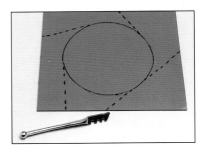

1. The dotted lines represent the suggested direction and angle of the scores. Start from one edge of the glass and move the score to meet the circle. Travel some way around the circle and then move the score away to another edge.

2. Place the pliers next to the score and break off the first pieces.

3. Move around the circle and continue to break off each section.

4. Use the pliers to "nip" off the sharp points. Grip the point with the tip of the pliers.

CUTTING A CURVE

Cutting a convex curve will require more than one score.

Make the first score following the line of the curve required. With great care make more scores within the curve. Make as many as you can close together. These inner scores can be tapped gently to loosen the tension and then break out these series of inner scores, with the pliers, removing them one at a time. Be cautious as you get further into the series of curves and if the scores still seem tight when you apply the pliers, resort to a little tapping to loosen them.

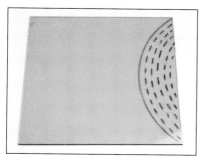

1. *The dotted lines represent the suggested score lines. Make a succession of scores inside the initial one. The deeper the curve the more you may need to make.*

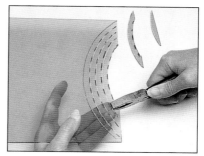

2. *Keep a steady hold on the glass with one hand. Use the pliers to gently but firmly "pull" out the scored sections.*

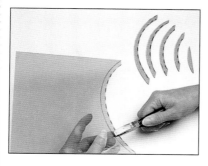

3. *As you become familiar with different glass, you will learn when it is best to use pliers or when tapping will be advantageous.*

USING A STRAIGHTEDGE

Using a straightedge is a method that requires some practice. It is also probably the only time that you will need to pull the cutter toward the body instead of away from you.

The trick of using a straightedge is to put enough pressure on the ruler to hold it steady while you are also putting pressure on the cutter while drawing it towards you and against the side of the ruler. The most common problem you will encounter is that the ruler will slip. A straightedge with a rubber backing will cling to the glass firmly and prevent it from moving while scoring.

TRANSPARENT GLASS

When cutting transparent glass, place the design or pattern on the work surface and the glass over the top. You can then cut directly onto the glass following visible lines of the pattern underneath.

OPALESCENT GLASS

As opalescent glass is not transparent you would normally use a light box. The pattern would be placed between the light box and the piece of glass. As opal glass does

transmit artificial light you will be able to see the pattern and can cut directly on to the glass following the lines underneath.

When cutting dense opal glass, use carbon paper to put the cut lines directly on the glass surface. Place a piece of carbon paper between the glass and the pattern. Using a fine pen or pencil, trace over the cut line on the pattern transferring the image on to the glass. Now cut directly on to the glass following the carbon line. If you do not have access to a light box, you will need to use templates (see below for advice on how to use these).

MIRRORED GLASS

Always cut mirrored glass on the reflective side. Protect the backing which is sensitive to scratching by brushing away any tiny glass shards on the work surface.

TEMPLATES

With opalescent glass or any glass that is not easy to see through you can also make templates if you don't have a light box handy. Templates are simply cut-out patterns of your design.

Transparent glass can be simply laid over the pattern ready for scoring.

Place a piece of paper over your design and trace it. Cut out the shapes accurately and lay them back on the design to check that they fit.

Place these templates on to the glass and draw around them with a felt tip pen or glass crayon. Now cut these shapes following the lines.

HEALTH AND SAFETY FOR GLASS CUTTING

✳ Always wear safety goggles to prevent injury from small glass fragments when cutting or grinding glass.

✳ Keep a first aid kit handy, and well stocked with plenty of plasters.

✳ Wear solid closed shoes and an apron to prevent small shards of glass sticking to your clothes or falling on your feet.

✳ Tiny particles of glass will flake off your cutting lines. These and other discarded offcuts should be regularly swept away with a brush. Do not be tempted to use the side of your hand. This simple action is the cause of most minor cuts.

✳ Keep only the pieces of glass you are using on the work surface. Do not allow discarded pieces and offcuts to accumulate in a pile. Discard or store them safely. Store larger pieces in a rack with dividers or a wooden bin. Smaller pieces can be stored in a wooden or plastic box or bin.

✳ Handle pieces of glass firmly and confidently. You are more likely to drop something you have not picked up properly.

✳ Extra care must be taken when handling a large or stock sheet piece of glass. Before handling, tap the glass gently with the ball end cutter. If it rattles, you may have a "run" or accidental crack in the sheet that can cause the sheet to break apart while you are moving it on the cutting

✳ Carry large sheets of glass in a vertical position. Use one hand to support the sheet from below and the other hand to steady the sheet from above. Wear protective gloves when handling large sheets of glass.

Lead Work

There are two parallel techniques used for assembling glasswork. Leading, the traditional method, is often associated with classic stained glass windows, while copper foil – a more contemporary approach – is identified with lampshades.

Both systems have their advantages and a working knowledge of each method is essential for glasswork today. Very often people will stay with whatever technique they learned first, thereby setting a limit on the development of their craft.

Lead channels

Leading is the traditional framework used to build up windows. Rumour has it that this technique was developed because the early glassmakers were not able to produce sheets of glass large enough to fill a window opening. Whatever the true origins of this technique, little has changed since the first leaded light was made from small pieces of glass held together with lead channels or cames. A lead came, which is either an H or U shape in profile, is generally available in 1.2–1.8 m (4–6-foot) lengths. Glass is fitted into the channel of the cames and these are then soldered together at the junctions.

Various-sized cames are used for window projects, depending upon both the size of the glass pieces and the size of the window itself. The centre of the came is known as the heart. Lead cames are available with either a flat or round surface. Cames come in different widths. The most common widths used are 5 mm, 6 mm, 9 mm and 13mm (^{3}/$_{16}$ inch, ^{1}/$_4$ inch, ^{3}/$_8$ inch and ^{1}/$_2$ inch). Deciding which came goes where is determined by a balance of both aesthetics and structure.

Most studios will have a preference for a particular style of leading and a lot of them select "round" lead as it seems to be stronger and less likely to distort while "leading up".

By application, lead cames must be flexible, malleable channels that can be formed around the various shapes of cut glass. Most lead manufactured today is extruded through a metal die and is usually at least 99 percent pure lead. The first concern of many beginners is how to transport this floppy, bending channel safely home without folding and kinking it into a useless mass of scrap. There are extreme cases of people arriving to purchase cames equipped with a 1.8 m (6-foot) length of board to keep the cames straight on the trip home. This overcaution is not necessary as all lead is straightened by stretching just prior to use. Ideally, lead should be used directly from the manufacturer's lead boxes. But most people find that coiling the lengths is a

perfectly safe and convenient method of transporting small amounts of came for future use.

HEALTH AND SAFETY WHEN WORKING WITH LEAD, COPPER FOIL, SOLDER, FLUX AND GLASS PAINTS

* Do not eat, drink, or smoke when working with stained glass.
* Keep food and beverages away from work surfaces and working area.
* Always wash hands thoroughly with soap and water after handling lead or solder and before eating or drinking.
* Always protect cuts or scratches on your hands or skin with plasters before working.
* Work in a well-ventilated area especially when soldering or working with patinas.
* Use a fan to blow away vapours during soldering or use a fume trap (available from stained glass suppliers).
* Wear an apron or protective clothing and wash these separately from your normal clothes.
* Wear safety glasses during cutting, grinding or soldering.
* Wear closed solid shoes.
* Wear protective gloves when using a patina.
* Keep glass and lead safely stored out of the reach of children and animals.
* Wear a mask when working with glass paints; these fine powdered paints can be easily inhaled and contain finely-ground glass, iron oxide and lead.
* Wear a mask that guards you from breathing in fumes when soldering.
* Wear a mask when sandblasting.
* Work on a sturdy, stable table at a comfortable working height (around waist level), and have access to a sink and running water.
* Have safe electrical outlets for soldering irons and glass grinders.
* Have a hard-surfaced easy-to-clean floor.
* Pregnant women should check with their GP before carrying out any stained glass work.

LEAD WORKING EQUIPMENT

There are several tools and materials that come into play when leading and below is an explanation of each of these to show how they fit into the process:

LEAD VICE

The vice is used to hold one end of the channel securely while the other end is pulled firmly to straighten and strengthen the came. Use a pair of pliers to help you; pull just enough to straighten the came without adding more than 2.5 cm (one inch) to the total length. Pull too hard and the came can either slip from the vice or snap in two, sending you backward to an uncertain fate. Remember that cames are stretched only once just prior to use.

LATHE OR FID

Available in many shapes, the lathe or fid opens the lead channel, allowing the glass to be positioned

Stretching the came with the lead vice and a pair of pliers.

within. Cames will distort while being worked into position and the channels must always be reopened to ease leading. After a came has been stretched, run the rounded end inside the channel, flaring it slightly outward. This tool will wear with use and should be "repointed" so that it will continue to reach inside and open the channel. We have found that the best lathes are handmade from a hard wood such as ash or oak and personalized to suit the hand.

LEAD KNIFE

Lead knives are used to cut the cames to size while the panel is being leaded together. There are two basic shapes available and which is best is just a matter of preference. The long

curved blade of the Don Carlos or the short, rounded blade of the standard knife both give a firm, crisp cut.

The rounded blade is moved from side to side as pressure is applied downward, cutting the came neatly with a minimal amount of distortion. A short putty knife with a rigid, nonflexing blade can be adapted for lead cutting with acceptable results. Most lead knives are available with a weighted end used for tapping horseshoe nails into position. Like any knife, the blade will dull with use and should be periodically resharpened on a whetstone. Dull knives tend to crush the lead, making it difficult or impossible to work with.

In addition to the lead knife some stained glass suppliers will stock came cutters or lead snips for cutting the lead. These can be comfortable and useful tools to use.

Horseshoe nails

Horseshoe nails are used while leading is in progress to hold the glass and lead in position. The flat-sided, sharp nail is less likely to damage the glass or lead than a conventional oval-shaped nail and they are easily removed as the leading progresses.

Cement

As you will soon notice, the glass will generally fit comfortably into the came leaving a generous gap alongside. Cementing the panel fills this space, making the window strong and weatherproof.

Most studios will purchase a ready-made cement especially made for leaded lights. However, this luxury can be avoided by making your own. Numerous recipes are available and this is but one.

Mix sash putty, white spirit, and plaster into a dense, creamlike liquid. Grate some charcoal into a fine powder and add to darken the mixture.

The cement is applied with a stiff brush strong enough to push the mixture into all the recesses of the lead channel.

How long the cement is left to dry on the panel is a matter of temperature and the type of cement itself. During warm weather, cement can set in a few hours, making removal the next day a nightmare of epic proportions. The cement should never be allowed to set firmly on the glass and lead.

Whiting

The whiting, or powdered chalk, is used

to absorb the excess oil from the cement, allowing the panel to become dry and clean. A softer brush is used to remove the cement and whiting.

SOLDER

An alloy of two metals, lead and tin, solder is melted with a soldering iron and is used for both copper foil and lead came projects. Sold by weight and graded by the ratio of lead to tin, it is recommened that you use a 50:50 mix. Solder

with a higher tin content will melt at a lower temperature and finish with a more silvery appearance.

Solder with a resin or flux core is intended only for electrical repair work and is best avoided. The same goes for plumber's solder, which is temptingly inexpensive because of the low tin content, but extremely unworkable when soldered to anything but copper piping.

Lead light cement

Lead vice

Lead knife

Stiff brush

Grate polish

Solder

Lead cames

Horseshoe nails

Hammer

Whiting

Tallow candle

Wire wool

Fid

Copper Foil

Copper foil is a thin tape with an adhesive back that is wrapped around the glass. The foiled pieces of glass are then soldered together in strong, delicate shapes or patterns.

When compared to lead cames, copper foil is a simpler technique requiring fewer steps and fewer materials to complete a project. However, the main attraction to foil work is its tremendous versatility in tackling a wide range of projects, from small window hangings to lampshades.

The copper foil method is attributed to the inventiveness of Louis Comfort Tiffany, whose name has always been associated with the delicate "Tiffany-style" lampshades and windows of the late 19th Century. Not content with the heavy, one-dimensional qualities of traditional lead cames, Tiffany's craftsmen cut thin strips of copper that were wrapped around the glass and then soldered together in complex patterns and shapes.

Like the lead came, the question of which size foil to use is a common question when beginning a project. One of the advantages of copper foil is the delicacy that can

be achieved and most people always use as narrow a foil as possible. However, narrow foil is more time-consuming to apply and is not suitable for all projects. Lampshades or windows with large pieces of glass will require wider foil that is stronger and that will maintain a rigid shape. Although most machine-made glass is 3 mm ($\frac{1}{8}$ inch) thick, antique or handmade glass can vary in thickness even within the sheet itself, which can necessitate using two different foil sizes on a single piece.

Various sizes of copper foil tape with hand crimpers and burnishers.

Copper foil is conveniently available in sealed bags ranging in size from 12 mm ($^5/_{12}$ inch) to 13mm ($^1/_2$ inch) widths suitable for all types of coloured glass. The few specialized tools used for copper foil were devised to remove some of the tedium of wrapping large quantities of glass in preparation for assembly.

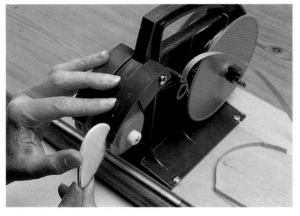

ABOVE *A copper foiling machine. This is worth investing in if you plan to make a lot of copper foil projects.*

FOILING MACHINE

A grooved, hard rubber roller centres and wraps the foil as the glass is pushed around. Although this type of machine requires practice, eventually the glass can be wrapped with much greater speed and accuracy than by hand. The machines are generally supplied with three interchangeable rollers, 5mm, 15mm and 3mm ($^3/_{16}$, $^7/_{12}$ and $^1/_8$ inch), being the most commonly used widths.

Electrically powered foiling machines are quicker still. The rubber wheel, activated by a foot switch, is driven by an electric motor.

FOIL CRIMPER

Whether you use a foiling machine or hand foil each piece, the foil must be folded and smoothed onto the sides of the glass to achieve a neat, strong bond. Although foiling machines often claim to burnish each piece as it is wrapped, in reality the foiled edges must be turned down or smoothed as a separate step. A crimper has a thin, flexible groove that – when run around the foiled edge – presses both these edges smooth against the glass with one action.

A flat piece of wood will also crimp the foil, one side at a time.

FINISHING PATINAS

After you have completed the assembly of your lampshade or panel made with soldered areas. Solder, like most metals, will oxidize and discolour in time, leaving a dull grey finish. High tin content solder will retain its lustre if treated with metal polish and some pieces do benefit aesthetically from this treatment. However, we have found that the dramatic contrast of glass and soldered lines is further highlighted by darkening the solder with a patina. All patinas work best when applied to the solder immediately after the project is complete. If you wait even a few hours, the solder will begin to oxidize, requiring a quick rubdown with a fine-grade wire wool or a wash with hot soapy water to achieve a bright finish. A patina finish will also brighten if rubbed with metal polish.

Copper sulphate crystals: A patina that leaves the soldered lines a coppery colour. Dissolve one tablespoon of the crystals in 120ml of hot water.

Black-it and copper-bright solution: These two chemicals are available as a premixed solution and will give a stronger and darker finish than copper sulphate. Black-it contains a trace amount of selenium oxide, an extremely strong chemical that demands care when used. It will blacken solder. Copper-bright turns the solder a copper colour. Always wear rubber gloves when working with any of the finishing patinas.

Finishing patinas, clockwise from top:black-it, copper-bright and copper sulphate crystals.

the copper foil technique there are several alternatives for finishing the

Soldering

To assemble the pieces of glass – whether they are leaded or foiled – you will need to use solder and a soldering iron. Soldering irons, like pliers, tend to be a household item that lie in wait, quietly rusting, until a small bit of electrical repair work requires them to be retrieved from the bottom of the tool drawer.

Unfortunately, the iron that many of us are able to borrow from a friend or locate in a drawer is seldom up to the job of soldering for glasswork. We have found that people who have trouble soldering are usually working with a tool that isn't appropriate for the job.

Nowadays, as a matter of convenience and safety, most studios work with electric- rather than gas-heated irons. The gas heats up the tip of the iron with an open flame and the iron requires a cylinder that takes up space and may well be against safety regulations.

SOLDERING IRONS AND HOW TO USE THEM

Irons of less than 75 watts do not retain enough heat to melt the amounts of solder that you will be using. When soldering, the iron is in constant use and the process will soon begin to dissipate the heat that has built up in the tip of the iron. Small irons with little heat retention will lose heat so quickly that the solder will stop flowing and become tacky and sluggish,

making joints weak and messy.

Irons of over 150 watts tend to be just too speedy for most work and have a tendency to burn or melt everything they come into contact with. Large wattage irons can be regulated by switching the power off when excessive heat causes meltdown, but this procedure is usually forgotten and you are left wondering why the iron has gone cold.

There are available, at a price, irons that seem to be made especially for glasswork that contain a temperature control unit built into the handle. The temperature is regulated by replaceable tips of various heat ranges and size. One temperature control iron in the 100–200 watt range can be used for delicate or heavy work by a simple exchange of tips.

At one time, irons were available only with massive copper tips that corroded and required constant reshaping with metal files. Most irons are now available with an iron-coated or plated tip giving a long life and ease of use. For most work, a screwdriver shaped tip measuring about 6 mm ($^1/_4$

inch) at its working end will give smooth, neat joints. Any metal that is constantly heated, cooled, and exposed to corrosive chemicals will soon show wear. No matter what iron you use, remove the tip frequently to prevent it from seizing in the barrel and eventually ruining the iron.

Impurities in solder and lead will cause carbon deposits to build up on the tip surface, greatly decreasing its ability to transfer heat to the work. Allow the iron to heat up to its working temperature and wipe the tip with a chemical cleaner or damp sponge until the tip is shiny. This process, known as "tinning," is repeated whenever the tip is discoloured with black carbon deposits. The coated tip, unlike the old solid copper ones, can never be filed or reshaped. Once the coating is damaged, the tip will rapidly begin to deteriorate. The manufacturer's instructions will always state something like: "Do not file coated tip" and you can be sure this is good advice.

After all the thought and deliberation about wattage, tip shape, coated or copper, temperature control, etc, there is one last item that is often overlooked. Buy a metal sand that is large enough to keep the iron from rolling off the table, setting fire to the carpet and perhaps spreading to the rest of your home. In addition to melting solder, irons are also excellent incendiary devices and when given the opportunity will burn any nearby combustible.

There is a range of soldering irons available for glasswork. Be sure to purchase a metal stand too, as soldering irons can quickly burn neighbouring items if left lying by themselves on a work table.

FLUX

Without flux the solder will not bond to the surface of lead or copper foil. It also acts to clean the metal, remove and prevent oxidization, and allow the solder to flow. There are a variety of fluxes available, both in liquid and solid form. Some are suitable for lead and others more suitable for copper foil. There are also liquid fluxes on the market that are suitable for both.

Soldering irons for glasswork with a metal stand

The oleic acid flux is an old standby but consult your local stained glass suppliers and check which flux they stock and recommend. Flux in a solid form for lead work, is called a tallow stick or candle.

Although tallow will clean the lead joint when heated by the iron, you will need to use a soft wire brush or wire wool just prior to fluxing to remove any oxidization that may have occurred. This will provide clean, shiny joints

ready for soldering.

Lead cames that are stored wrapped in newspaper or boxed will remain free of oxidization and will be easier to solder. Unlike lead cames that are soldered only at junctions, copper foil projects are soldered along the entire seam. Just like cames, soldering is always a quicker, smoother process if the foil has not been allowed to discolor or oxidize.

Rolls of copper foil that are stored in the original packaging will remain clean and free of oxidization and ready for use. Don't leave foiled glass lying around for too long before

soldering, as the foil will tarnish. The active ingredient in most commercial fluxes is zinc chloride, a corrosive, toxic chemical that, while being an effective flux, is a very unpleasant material to work with.

Most people use only nontoxic, water-based fluxes that do not emit harmful fumes or corrode the soldering tips. Use sparingly and flux only the areas you will be soldering immediately, as flux evaporates and leaves residues on the foil that will affect the process.

As bottles of flux have a habit of frequently falling over and soaking everything around, pour a small amount into an open-top container for immediate use and keep the rest safely bottled.

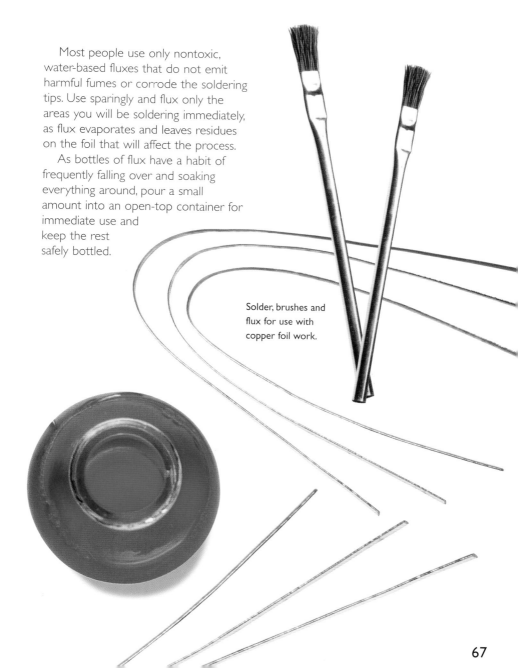

Solder, brushes and flux for use with copper foil work.

HOW TO SOLDER

Soldering affects both the appearance and strength of a piece and is an important aspect of any project. Whether you are working with copper foil or lead, your soldering success will depend on having an iron of adequate wattage with a clean, tinned tip ready to melt solder. Turn the iron on and when hot wipe with either a damp sponge or chemical tip cleaner to remove blackened deposits. Brush the tip with flux and then melt a touch of solder onto it. The iron should readily melt the solder so that the working area of the tip is covered with a shiny coating of solder. Irons that are blackened by the impurities from lead and solder will not transmit heat efficiently to the working area, regardless of the wattage.

Lead channels

Small gaps where the channels meet can be filled or packed by cutting off the bottom of a small wedge of lead and inserting the "T" into the gap. Once you are satisfied that all the gaps have been filled, it is often helpful to give the joints a quick cleaning with a fine wire brush to remove any oxidization. Hold the solder on the joint and allow the iron to melt a neat pool of solder. A few moments is usually long enough to solder the lead into a strong, neat joint. If the iron is not hot enough the solder will appear lumpy and irregular; if too hot, the iron can melt away the lead channel itself. Be careful! Don't be concerned about the heat of the iron cracking the glass.

Copper foil

Copper foil is soldered along the entire length of the adjoining sections of glass. As with lead, copper foil that has been oxidized will be difficult to solder and it is advisable to keep your foiled pieces protected in a plastic bag if there is a delay of a day or more before you are ready to solder. There are three soldering techniques employed when working with copper foil.

HOW TO SOLDER COPPER FOIL

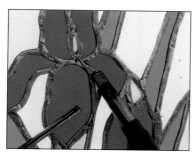

Tinning or flat soldering:
The inside seams of most copper foil projects are soldered with just a smooth or flat seam of solder. Flux the copper foil with a brush and begin soldering by flowing just enough solder to coat the seam and fill in any gaps; although you can form a "bead" of solder directly to the copper foil, sometimes it is more useful to tin the seams first and then to bead the outside areas afterwards on top of the tinned seams. This is particularly advisable when you are building up three-dimensional projects.

Tack soldering: To prevent pieces
from moving out of position by the very action of soldering, use a small blob of solder to hold the glass in place. Apply flux with a brush at key junctions and then melt a small amount of solder to hold the pieces together. Tack soldering is also essential with three-dimensional projects to hold the shape temporarily in position before going on to the next step.

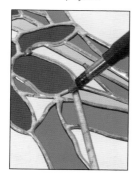

Bead soldering: This process is generally applied to
the outside of the finished project. Apply flux to the complete seam and slowly move the iron along the seam while feeding in solder to either the top or side of the tip. Work slowly, moving the iron only as fast as it is able to melt the solder. You should allow the solder to build up until it forms a domed or rounded smooth seam. Flux only a small area at a time, as the flux itself will evaporate. Moving the iron too quickly is the most common problem for beginners, and learning to form a smooth, neat bead can sometimes take a little practice.

Painting Glass

Glass painting has been used to illustrate and decorate leaded glass windows throughout the centuries. Exquisite artistry created draping folds of fabric, faces rich with expression, and flora and fauna alike.

EQUIPMENT

There are certain tools that are required for glass painting. However, you can improvise, and in some cases ordinary artists' brushes will work if you are unable to purchase the specialized ones.

Not all glass artists have a kiln of their own. Professional studios will often rent out their kiln for an hourly fee. Or contact a local college and inquire if there is a kiln available on the same basis.

GLASS PALETTE

This is to provide a surface for mixing the paints. You will need a square of thick, clear glass preferably sandblasted to provide an abrasive surface for mixing the paint powder. A palette knife is useful for mixing the paint.

Painting on glass is an exacting technique and is very different from many other forms of pictorial painting. Paint for glass is a mixture of powdered oxides that are ground and mixed with water and gum arabic. Much of the technique lies in not just applying the paint but also removing it to create texture and shading. The finished work is fired in a kiln to fuse the paint to the glass.

ABOVE A painted and leaded medieval window copied from the St. Eustace window in Chartres, France.

TOOLS FOR PAINTING GLASS

Gum arabic

BRUSHES

Liner, rigger or tracer: Long-haired brushes, which are soft, flexible and have a slender point. They are used with trace paint for tracing outlines and delicate work.

Mop or wash brush: A round soft brush for holding enough paint to apply a wash.

Badger: A thick, very soft, long-haired brush for matting or shading colour.

Hoghair brush or scrub: A stiff short-haired brush for stippling paint before it has been fired.

Stippler

OTHER EQUIPMENT

Toothpicks: or sharp-pointed bamboo sticks are useful for picking away the paint.

Armrest: For resting your wrist while leaving your hand free over the glass, you will do well to employ an arm support. This can easily be made from a narrow strip of wood with a small block of wood glued to each end.

Badger brush

Hoghair brush

Trace brushes

Mop brushes

Palette knife

PAINTING GLASS

MATERIALS

Trace paint

A dark paint used for outlines and details in line form. If used correctly it can block out light completely. Trace paint is mixed with water and gum arabic. The gum arabic is a setting medium and enables the paint to adhere to the glass.

Trace paint is applied with a tracer or rigger. You must apply the paint in one continuous stroke with the brush. Once the paint has dried (which is very quickly) you must not go back and apply more paint over the line. If you do, it will "fry" when it is fired; ie the two overlying areas of paint will separate when heated and bubble. You must also not retouch the line that has been painted. Once the trace line is dry you can use a toothpick or bamboo stick to remove excess paint. Literally scrape off what you don't want. Trace paint is fired at about 620°C (1150°F). This will probably vary from kiln to kiln.

Shading colour

Used for shadowing, shading colour creates tone and texture. It is generally mixed with water and a drop of gum arabic and is applied with a soft brush or "mop" over the entire area on which you are working. It is then stippled or worked on with various brushes to create a particular tone, shadow or texture.

Many different effects can be created with shading colour once it is applied. It is also applied over trace paint and usually after the trace paint has been fired. Shading colour can be used alone and is fired in the same way as trace paint. Shading colour and trace paint fire to a lighter tone.

Silver stain

Silver stain is the misleading name given to glass stains that produce yellow to amber colours after firing. Stain will change the colour of glass, unlike paint, which simply covers it. Stain is mixed with water and is usually applied to the back of the glass – the opposite side to trace paint and shading colour. Silver stain

contains silver nitrate and has corrosive properties.

Don't use the same brushes and palette as you do for paints. Always wash the brushes and equipment immediately, and avoid contact with skin. Some glass will not accept silver stain so care must be taken when choosing the type of glass to be stained. A good idea is to test a piece first and keep a record for future reference. Stains fire at approximately 601°C (1110°F).

Always clean the glass thoroughly before painting with a little of the paint itself. Allow to dry, then wipe the paint off with a clean rag.

FIRING COLOURS IN A KILN

Kiln working and painting is a special subject and here we are able to give only a very basic introduction to their use. If you are interested in finding out more about this subject we suggest you consult a book that deals only with painting on glass.

The high temperature used in the kiln allows the paint and glass to fire together forming a single decorative surface that is permanent. There are many types of glass kilns available, from small units that fire single pieces of glass to large batch-type kilns capable of firing many pieces at one time. All glass kilns must have a controllable temperature range up to a minimum of 657°C (1200°F).

A lot of people use a propane gas-fired top loader, which usually prove to be efficient, quick and trouble-free. Electric kilns are also widely used, although we have found them to require more time to complete a firing cycle. Some kilns have a digital temperature control unit that allows you to programme a firing cycle. The pieces are placed painted side up onto a smooth, level bed of whiting (calcium carbonate or plaster of Paris), which prevents the glass from fusing with the kiln itself. After you have selected the appropriate temperature, the kiln is fired. At the end of firing you simply turn off the kiln and allow the glass to cool slowly or anneal. Do not open the kiln while it is still hot, or you will be greeted by the gentle pop of cracking glass as the cold air rushes in.

Sand Blasting

Don't be deterred from experimenting with sandblasting just because you don't have ready access to a sandblaster. Most well-equipped studios will have a machine that they may be willing to rent out at an hourly rate.

Alternatively, they might be persuaded to sandblast other people's work for a set charge per square foot. Phone around and be persistent!

The sandblasting unit consists of four basic elements that all work together. The air compressor is the motor of the unit and provides compressed air to the sand-mixing unit. The pressurized sand is then forced through a flexible pipe into a sealed cabinet where it exits through a gun fitted with a small nozzle. An extractor fan attached to the cabinet removes excess sand and maintains clear visibility while sandblasting.

Insert your hands into the long rubber gloves that are sealed where they enter the cabinet to position the glass and control the sand jet. Always wear a mask when sandblasting.

RESIST

The preparation and application of the resist is the main skill of sandblasting. The resist protects the glass surface from the abrasive power of the pressurized sand. Areas left exposed to the sand jet will be abraded or frosted. Transparent resist is a heavy grade of adhesive film with a paper backing that is peeled away. We have used ordinary sticky-back vinyl with good results, although the clear resist is both stronger and easier for transferring a design onto the glass.

Glass Appliqué

Glass appliqué is similar to fabric appliqué, where a pattern or picture is built up from small scraps of material sewn onto a larger piece.

The application of glass onto glass is a technique that involves neither lead nor copper foil. Basically, scraps of glass are glued onto a glass panel and the gaps in between are grouted. The glass pieces can be literally scrap shapes, or you can cut them according to your design. The end result can be abstract or you can form a definite picture or pattern with the glass.

Apart from the obvious glass-cutting tools, and wet and dry paper for polishing the edges of cut pieces, you will need silicone adhesive, and black Universal stainer to mix with white interior filler to form a "grout".

Designing Your Own Stained Glass

Designing your own stained glass patterns can be immensely satisfying and is not as difficult as you might think. To begin with, most people gain their experience from copying ideas and using templates in books. The next step is to design your own patterns and pictures. Inspiration for design concepts can come from almost anywhere – books, magazines the natural world around you, a child's drawing – the list is virtually endless. This chapter looks at how to translate these ideas into an actual stained glass project, to avoid certain pitfalls, and to produce an item that you are proud of and pleased with.

Designing Your Own Stained Glass

There are many stained glass pattern books on the market for beginners and advanced students alike. There are also many books with pictures of contemporary and traditional stained glass windows that will give you inspiration.

However, most people will find themselves developing their own ideas as their skills improve and, inevitably, will want to create their own designs.

When designing or developing concepts to be made from glass, certain limitations are imposed due to the restrictions of the material. Sometimes this can work to your advantage because you are forced to think further than just the picture on the paper. Adding extra lines or sections of glass to balance the strength of the project could enhance the design unexpectedly.

With lead and copper foil being the "skeleton" of the piece in terms of holding the glass together, these lines should be considered an integral part of the design and can be utilized as such.

Ideas can, and will, come from many different sources. Consider adapting a drawing or a design from paintings, interesting graphics, architectural details and magazine features, depending on your particular style or taste and

ABOVE *This window has been translated using the glass appliqué technique, Friebel College, London.*

whether the image is figurative or linear. Colour balance will play an important part in the appearance and effect of the finished piece. When you are working with transparent glass, hold it up to the light and consider the colour, texture and "light play" as the sun shines through the glass.

Most studios will have a light box on which to lay pieces of glass to see how one colour appears against another. This works well for both opalescent and transparent glass. A light box can also be useful to trace the pattern through on to the glass and eliminate the need for templates.

For transparent glass, an easel is the most effective method of displaying your choice of colours, but as this is a large piece of equipment to have in your home, you may prefer to stick small pieces of glass with adhesive putty to a window pane. This will provide the same answers and will enable you to see where one colour may overpower another.

MAKING A SELECTION

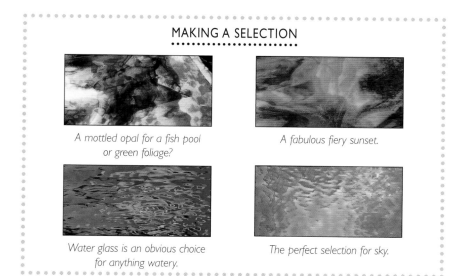

A mottled opal for a fish pool
or green foliage?

A fabulous fiery sunset.

Water glass is an obvious choice
for anything watery.

The perfect selection for sky.

Once you have formulated a concept for a design, draw it out on paper. Measure a perimeter and plan the design within it. Look at it and decide if some of the shapes are too small or impossible to cut. Alter it accordingly. Keep the design simple and avoid any difficult cuts. You will build up more confidence by designing and executing a simple pattern, rather than overwhelming yourself with a complicated one.

While designing the panel, consider its strength. A design with smaller pieces of glass will be stronger than a panel with a few large sections that do not intersect. Avoid a long line of glass that travels from one side of the panel to the other. Unless divided in some way with your design line, a narrow section of glass will be a vulnerable part of the panel and could break.

Once you have modified your drawing for cutting and you are satisfied with the effect, ink it in and make at least two or three copies. Whether you are working in lead or foil, you will always need one copy for cutting from and one copy to check that your pieces fit. It is important that you work in a sense of order with glass. Unnecessary breakages and minor cuts can occur if your table is messy.

Consider the streaks and colour variations in the choice of glass available. Use these selections to your advantage. Illustrate a cloudy sky with a streaky blue. Mottled green may suit foliage on a tree. Water glass could not be a better choice than for water.

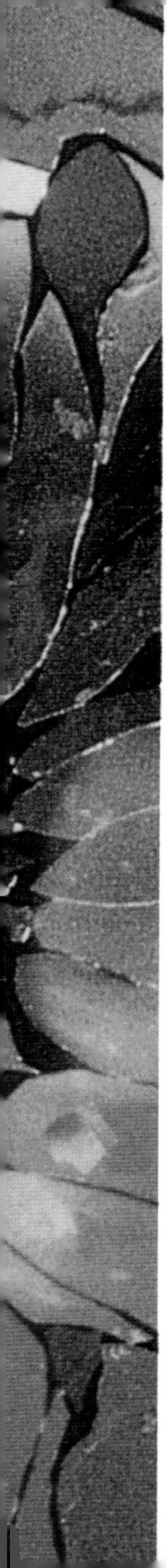

Projects

The projects illustrated over this next chapter use five different techniques:

* Copper foil
* Leading
* Appliqué
* Sandblasting
* Glass painting

Using Copper Foil

Copper foil is a versatile medium for holding pieces of glass together. Its flexibility from both the practical point of view and the opportunity for design give the stained glass worker enormous potential.

Tiny pieces of glass can be wrapped with the foil and soldered together to form the most intricate details. Three-dimensional forms can be developed with more dexterity than with lead.

Some glass artists have a personal preference for working with either lead or foil, but when choosing to make items such as lampshades, boxes, or jewellery, copper foil would be the practical choice.

WILD IRISES PANEL

You will need
. . . .

* Various colours of semi-antique or cathedral glass
* glass cutter
* grozier and running pliers
* electric grinder or carborundum stone
* 5.5-mm ($^7/_{32}$-inch) copper foil
* fid
* solder
* soldering iron
* flux and brush
* patina

I *Compare the various colours of glass for balance and harmony.*

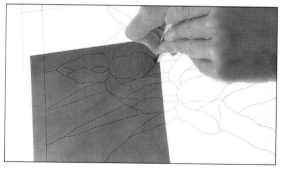

2 *The glass is transparent so it can be laid directly onto the design to be cut. (The pattern appears on page 144). Remember to always make at least two copies of the design, one to cut from and one to lay the pieces on for fitting. Cut the shapes from an area that will limit wastage. Allow a small margin from the shape and the edge of the glass. Start the score from just inside the edge of the glass.*

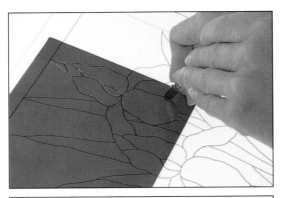

3 Score several pieces ready for breaking.

4 Using the ball end of the glass cutter, tap underneath the scored line to assist a tricky curved line to break.

5 Break the pieces with the pliers.

6 Hold the glass firmly with the fingers and thumb of the other hand.

7 Use the pliers to groz off sharp points.

8 Grind the edges of the glass on the electric grinding machine. Check that it is filled with water for lubricating the wheel. (If you don't have access to an electric grinder, use a carborundum stone.)

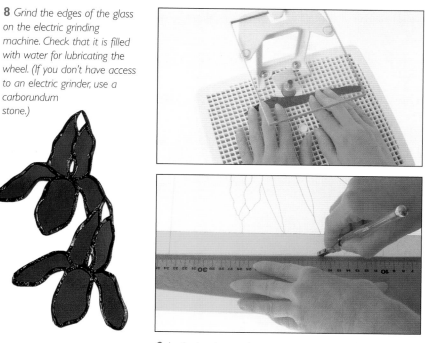

9 As the borders are long, narrow strips, you will need to use the straight edge to cut them.

10 The running pliers are useful to help break these long straight lines. Place the pliers with the raised section under the score and press the pliers together.

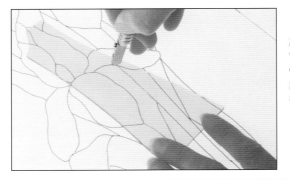

11 *Score the yellow glass following the direction of the vertical lines and then score the curves. Break the pieces with the pliers. Grind all the edges smooth.*

12 *Wash all the pieces before foiling each one.*

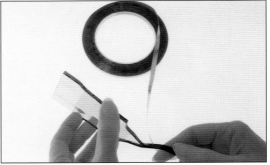

13 *Rub the foil down onto the glass. If you don't have a fid or crimper, use a small piece of wood or a pencil.*

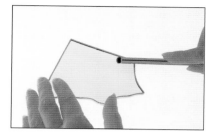

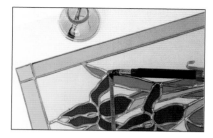

14 *Continue to do this, flattening the foil folded onto the sides of the glass and rubbing it down well.*

15 *Assemble the copper foiled pieces and apply the flux. Tuck solder the panel together to prevent the pieces from moving around.*

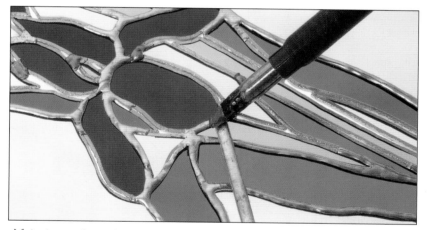

16 *Apply more flux and bead solder the front side of the panel. Turn the panel over and tin the back.*

17 *Hold the panel in a vertical position to tin the edges. Apply patina to the panel with a sponge and then wash it thoroughly with hot water and detergent.*

Flat-panelled Lamp

You will need

* * various opalescent glass: pale amber, red, blue and green
* * pencil and ruler
* * glass cutter
* * grozier and running pliers
* * carborundum stone
* * 5-mm ($^7/_{32}$-inch) copper foil
* * fid
* * solder
* * soldering iron
* * flux and brush
* * patina
* * vase cap and hoop
* * bulb holder and chain
* * lamp base

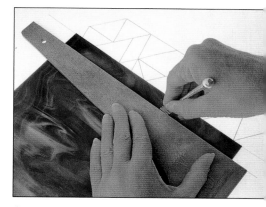

1 *Following the pattern on page 145, extend the diagonal lines with a pencil and ruler, as shown. Align the glass, and use a straight edge. Position the wheel of the cutter directly in line with the extended lines of the pattern.*

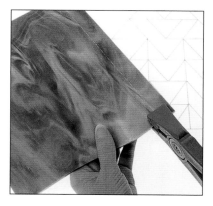

2 *Score, then break the piece away with running pliers.*

3 *Place the strip back on the pattern and trim the end to shape by following the line of the design.*

4 Continue to measure and score the glass in blocks of colour, using the geometry of the design as a guide.

5 The red is cut into strips then divided into triangles. Break these small pieces apart using the pliers held next to the score in one hand and gripping the glass firmly with the fingers of the other hand.

6 Continue cutting to build up the pattern.

7 Rub the edges of the glass with the stone, wash and foil the pieces, placing them back on the pattern as you work.

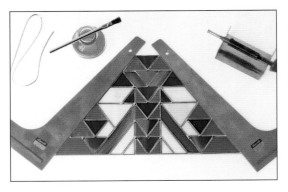

8 Use two straightedges to keep the sides of the panel straight. This is important as the final assembly will be dependent on the sides being perfectly straight.

9 *Flux and tack solder the copper seams together, then solder the panel together by fluxing and tinning both sides. Add more solder to one side only and form a beaded seam. The beaded side of the panel will be the outside of the lamp shade.*

10 *Each panel should be of exactly the same properties and identical. Continue to check as you work.*

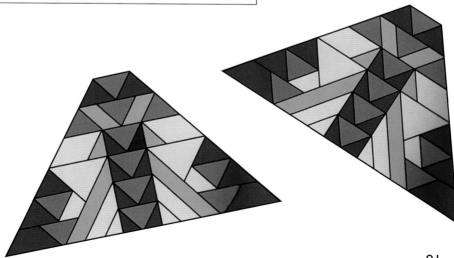

11 *When all the panels are complete, hold two together, checking that the top and bottom are level. If you do not have anyone to help or assist you with holding them in place while you solder, use a jig. (Make a jig with two pieces of wood trim nailed onto a wooden board. Nail one along one side of the board and another at a right angle along the adjacent side. This will now help to keep the lampshade's shape as well as assist with holding it steady while you solder it together.)*

12 *Do the same on the other two panels and when all four panels are tacked into place, tin the seams.*

13 *Turn the shade over and tin the inside seams.*

14 *Lift the shade and support it so that the long seams are as near to a horizontal position as possible. Bead solder along these edges and remember to flux as you go.*

15 *Attach a vase cap by fluxing and soldering it to the four main seams. The vase cap can then be tinned with solder. When all the soldering is complete wash the shade with detergent and hot water to remove flux and oil. Wearing rubber gloves, apply a patina with a sponge and then rinse and wash the shade thoroughly once again.*

TIFFANY-STYLE LAMP

The name of Louis Comfort Tiffany is most commonly associated with the many glass lampshades that his studios produced in the late 19th century. In fact, his shades are probably better known than his wonderful window designs. The intricacy of a curved Tiffany-style shade fascinates many people, but they are made from small pieces of flat glass assembled over a curved form.

With the aid of prepatterned commercial molds available to buy, constructing a shade can be a rewarding and surprisingly easy project. There are many designs to choose from and most are copies of Tiffany's originals. Accurate cutting and patience are the keys to success.

The kits come with one section or two, depending on the pattern of the complete dome. The design is already printed on the sections as a guide. Included are templates for you to cut out and use as a guide for cutting the glass. As you cannot see through opalescent glass, you will need these templates to lay on the glass for drawing around prior to cutting. Designs can range from simple to stunningly ornate. Some of the more complex designs can be enhanced with filagrees soldered to the finished shade. These are available from the suppliers along with the molds. Unprinted molds are also available for those who prefer to design their own lampshades.

You will need

* opal glass in white and yellow
* Opal (opalescent) glass in green/blue shades for the background
* mold for shade
* scissors
* glass cutter
* grozier pliers
* carborundum stone
* 6-mm ($^1/_4$-inch) or 5.5-mm ($^7/_{32}$-inch) copper foil (depending on thickness of glass)
* fid
* "tacky wax"
* solder
* soldering iron
* flux and brush
* patina
* lamp base

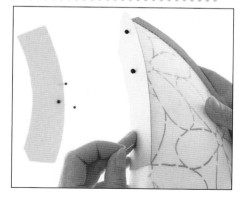

I *Cardboard "shoulders" are pinned to either side of the mold to keep the pieces of glass in line.*

2 *Cut out the templates carefully and check them against the design on the pattern.*

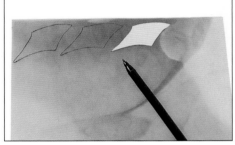

3 *Place the templates on the glass; try to keep the streaks or grain of the glass running in the same direction. Mark around the templates with a felt-tip pen or glass crayon.*

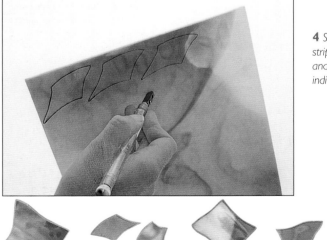

4 *Score and break this strip off before scoring and breaking the individual shapes of glass.*

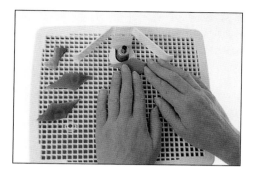

5 File each piece on a grinding machine or carborundum stone. Wash the pieces in preparation for foiling.

6 Now check the pieces of glass against the pattern.

7 Copper foil each piece. Place the glass in the centre of the foil, pressing gently. Check that there is an equal amount of foil left on each side and fold this down onto the sides of the glass. Rub down the foiled pieces with a fid or similar instrument.

8 Stick some "tacky wax" behind each piece of glass and assemble all the foiled pieces in their correct places on the form. Press each piece firmly so that they are secure.

9 Apply flux and tack solder the pieces together. Continue to flux and solder all the seams, then bead solder the outer seams. Carefully lift this section off the form.

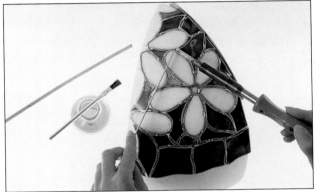

10 Place two interconnecting sections together and tack solder.

11 *Continue until you have a completed dome.*

12 *Run solder along the joining seams and attach a vase cap to the aperture. Flux and tin the vase cap and join the vase to the shade at the same time via the vertical seams.*

13 *Complete the soldering by beading the seams, attaching the vase cap on the inside of the lamp and tinning the inside. Wash the lamp well with hot water and detergent to remove all oil and flux residue.*

14 *Apply some patina with a sponge (always wear rubber gloves). Gently rub along all the solder seams and then repeat the washing process.*

Using Leading

Leading is the traditional technique for making stained glass windows. Strips of lead cames – with a channel down each side to accommodate the glass – are used as the basic skeleton of the window. Not only does the lead hold the pieces of glass together but its linear quality makes it an integral part of the overall design.

Now known as cames and sold in lengths of 1.8 m (6 feet) and in a variety of widths, these strips of lead were once more commonly known as "calmes."

ABOVE *"Syncopation," a geometric leaded window.*
Mathew Lloyd Winder

ABOVE *"Phototropism"*
Mathew Lloyd Winder

ABOVE *This leaded window uses more than 20 different types of glass.*
Mathew Lloyd Winder

TULIP PANEL

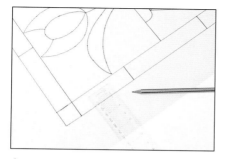

1 *Draw the design, following the pattern on page 147, and make three identical copies. Be sure to draw the lines using a felt-tip pen that marks a line the thickness of the heart of the lead. Usually this will be 2 mm ($^1/_{16}$ inch). Measure and draw an extra line of 6 mm ($^1/_4$ inch) on the inside of the overall measurement. This will indicate the centre of the 13-mm ($^1/_2$-inch) lead that will be used on the outside of the panel. Mark in this line with the felt-tip pen.*

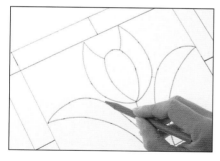

2 *As the glass is so narrow between the tulip and the leaf, you run the risk of it breaking. Make a small mark to indicate where it can be broken intentionally. The lead from the tulip and the leaf will touch at this point and cover the break.*

You will need
. . . .

* **✳** rolled cathedral glass in 4 colours
* **✳** felt-tip pen
* **✳** glass cutter
* **✳** grozier pliers
* **✳** 6 mm ($^1/_4$ inch) H channel lead came
* **✳** 13mm ($^1/_2$ inch) H channel lead came
* **✳** horseshoe nails
* **✳** solder
* **✳** soldering iron
* **✳** tallow candle or a suitable liquid flux and brush
* **✳** wire wool
* **✳** lead cement
* **✳** whiting powder
* **✳** brush for scrubbing lead
* **✳** fid for opening channels and cleaning lead
* **✳** wooden board and battens
* **✳** grate polish (optional)

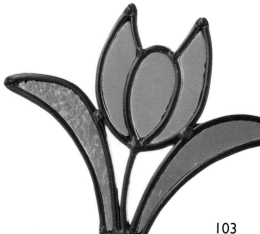

103

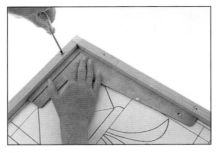

3 Place the pattern on a wooden board and screw or nail down two wooden strips to form right angles. These should be placed next to the external lines on the pattern.

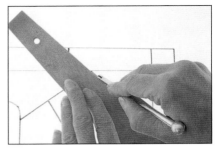

4 Score the glass on the inside of the 2-mm ($^1/_{16}$-inch) lines. Accurate cutting is very important, or the glass will not fit.

5 Align the cutting wheel with the inside of the line and use the straightedge to score the straight lines.

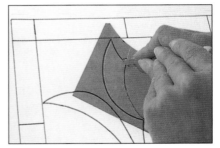

6 Score the curved tulip, taking the vertical lines from one edge of the glass to the other. Return to score the short inner curves.

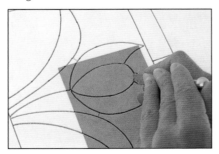

7 Score following the vertical lines first. Then score across the top of the tulip.

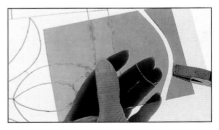

8 Place the edge of the pliers next to the score and support the glass firmly with the other hand. Grip the glass with the pliers and break the score.

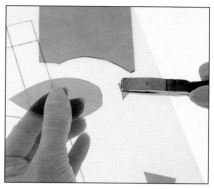

9 Tap directly underneath the scores with the ball end of the cutter. Remove any sharp points with the pliers by grozing the edges.

10 Nibble away any small slivers by gripping them with the pliers and nipping them off.

11 Lay all the pieces onto the pattern to check for accuracy. There should be a gap of 2 mm ($^1/_{16}$ inch) between each piece of glass.

12 Make sure the lead is stretched prior to use. Cut some lead longer than is required and mitre the end with the lead knife. Place the lead knife on top of the lead and press directly downwards, rocking the knife from side to side as you go.

13 Using the fid, open the lead channel. (If the lead has become flattened, open it with the lead knife.)

14 Place the outer lead on the pattern, making sure it fits into the corners. Measure and mark the lead for the next mitre.

15 Start from inside the right angle and place the glass in the lead channels. Place the lead and glass alternatively. Help the glass to slide in further by tapping it with a small piece of wood placed next to the side of the glass. If the glass has been cut accurately this is not a necessity, but where some pieces prove to be a tight fit, a light tap can help.

16 Measure and mark the lead with the knife before cutting. Each piece of lead should meet the flange of the adjoining lead and an allowance should be made for the width of the adjoining lead.

17 Hold the glass and lead in place as you work with horseshoe nails. Protect the glass by pushing scraps of lead in between the nails and glass.

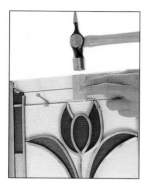

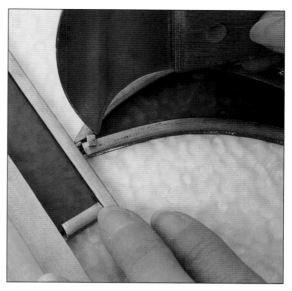

18 *Continue with the pattern, pushing the glass into the channels. (Protect the glass with a piece of wood as you tap it into its place.)*

19 *When the panel has been leaded, inevitably there will be slight gaps between the intersections. These can be filled using slivers of lead packed or pushed into the holes.*

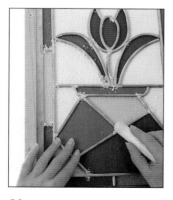

20 *Rub tallow candle flux on to the joints to be soldered.*

21 *Solder at the junctions on both sides. Be careful, as too much heat can cause the came itself to melt. Lift the iron off almost as soon as it has made contact with the lead.*

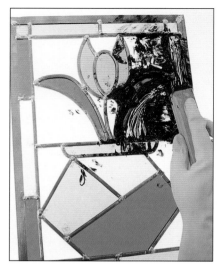

22 *Apply the cement with a hard brush, pushing it under the cames.*

23 *Scatter whiting over the panel. Allow the cement to partly dry, then remove the excess cement from around the cames with a fid.*

24 *Brush the panel vigorously. The whiting will absorb the oil from the cement and clean the glass. The leads will darken slowly as you continue to brush. To darken the cames further apply some grate polish. Turn over and repeat the process.*

LEADED LIGHT WINDOW

This window panel has been made to fit into a specific door frame. The same simple design could be adapted to fit any other door or window frame. Take care to protect the panel when fitting it back into the frame. Careless hammering of the beading could crack the glass.

1 *Take out the beading or scrape out the putty from the rebate of the door or window and measure the opening for the width and height. Subtract 2 mm ($^1/_{16}$ inch) from the height and the width and then draw out the pattern (see page 148). Subtracting this from the overall measurement will give some room for the window to be comfortably "fitted" into the opening of the door.)*

Make two copies of the original pattern. Draw all the lines with a felt-tip pen the width of the central channel of the lead. Make an additional line 19 mm ($^3/_4$ inch) from the inside of the external measurement. As the outer piece of lead is to be 13 mm ($^1/_2$ inch) in width, this additional line will indicate where to cut the glass that will fit into this lead.

Lay the pattern on a large board and nail down battens at right angles in one corner, next to the outer lines of the design. (The battens should extend beyond the length of the vertical and horizontal outer lines.) Cut out all the glass, leaving the 2-mm ($^1/_{16}$-inch) gap for the lead between each piece. Measure and cut two strips of the 13-mm ($^1/_2$-inch) lead and lay them on the inside of the battens. Measure to the required length on the pattern and mitre or butt joint the ends.

2 *Start placing or slotting the pieces of cut glass into the channels of the lead, separating each of the pieces with another piece of 6-mm ($^1/_4$-inch) lead. Take care to measure each piece and make an allowance for the next strip of lead that will lay alongside.*

3 A gentle tap with a piece of wood will help the glass sink into the lead heart. This is not always necessary, but it may help if the piece of glass is just a fraction over the line.

4 Place the glass and lead alternately. Measure and cut the lead to allow space for the corresponding strip.

5 When the panel is complete, rub tallow flux onto the intersections. If the lead has oxidized, rub each intersection first with a little wire wool or wire brush. Melt only enough solder at each junction to cover and join where the lead cames meet.

6 After the panel has been soldered at the junctions on both sides, brush cement into the gaps between the glass and the cames. Turn the panel over and repeat the cementing. This process will strengthen and weatherproof the panel.

7 Sprinkle some whiting onto the glass and cames. This will help to absorb the oil from the cementing and also clean the glass.

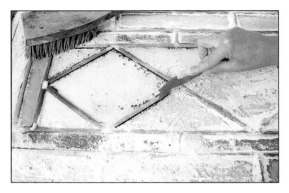

9 Brush the panel vigorously to remove excess cement and powder from the glass and the cames. The cames will darken with continued brushing but adding some black grate polish will help to darken the cames further.

8 Allow the cement to partly dry. Use a fid or wooden stick to remove excess cement from the cames.

11 If the window does not fit easily, or is slightly out of line, trim the external lead with a sharp lead knife. Just removing a sliver of lead may be all that's required to allow the window to fit. Replace the beading or putty the glass in place.

10 Sit the lower section of the glass into the opening of the frame and against the rebate. Carefully push the window back to rest against the rest of the rebate.

Using Appliqué

The application of glass onto glass is a straightforward technique that does not involve lead or copper foil.

A panel or window is created either by using leftover scraps of glass, or glass cut to a specified design. The pieces are then glued to a panel of 3- or 6-mm ($^1/_8$- or $^1/_4$-inch) clear glass. Black or gray "grout" is used to fill the areas in between the glass. This technique offers a great deal of freedom and creativity.

LEFT *These bright and striking pheasants in a golden wheatfield are fabricated using colour appliqué with painted detail*
Froebel College, London

LEFT *A woodland scene with flamboyant bluebells and foxgloves are created from glass appliqué.* **Froebel College, London**

LEFT *The versatility of glasswork is amply demonstrated in this wonderful appliqué window featuring little birds, foliage and bright blue sky*
Froebel College, London

Vase of Flowers

You will need
* * * * * * * * * * * * *

* 6-mm (⅛-inch) clear glass (cut to required size of panel)
* assortment of coloured glass pieces
* felt-tip pen
* glass pliers
* grozier pliers
* carborundum stone
* silicone adhesive
* Universal stainer
* interior plaster filler

1 *Consider the glass you have available and if necessary cut some into specific shapes. For example, the tulip was cut following a small sketch while the glass stems were formed from existing pieces.*

2 *Cut the vase from the largest piece of glass available.*

3 Lay the pieces onto plain glass cut to size. Use sticky pads or adhesive putty to fasten down the glass as you work, cutting or selecting pieces the appropriate size or colour.

4 To fill the gaps between pieces you can lay glass over the shape and mark it with a felt-tip pen prior to cutting.

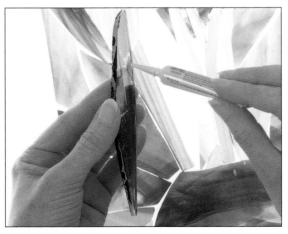

6 Mix black Universal stain into some interior filler then add water. Keep the consistency thick.

5 Apply adhesive to the back of each piece and press it firmly onto the glass. Allow to dry thoroughly. Take care to cover the glass completely with the glue to prevent the filler from seeping underneath.

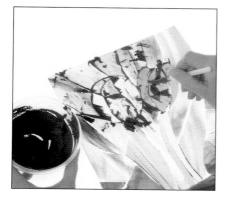

7 *Fill the gaps between the glass with this mixture.*

8 *Work your way down the panel, "grouting" the glass.*

9 *Allow the mixture to dry, then wipe away the excess from the surface.*

10 *Rub the surface of the grout with wire wool to smooth it. If desired, this whole process can be repeated again to raise the surface of the grout with the level of the glass.*

Using Sandblasting

Sandblasting is the technique of removing or abrading a glass surface.

The process of sandblasting is not far removed from spray painting except colour is removed rather than added from flashed or mirrored glass. It will create an etched surface giving a frosted appearance on transparent or clear coloured glass.

LEFT AND ABOVE *These stunning leaded panels have been decorated using deep sandblasting and acid polishing.*

FROSTED VASE

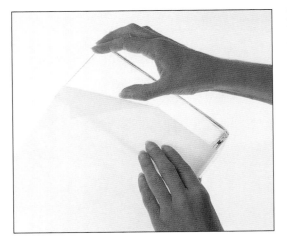

1 *Cut a piece of resist, large enough to surround the vase. Clean the vase thoroughly and, pulling back a corner of the film, stick down the adhesive film onto the glass. Rub the film smooth and try to avoid air bubbles forming underneath.*

2 *Slowly continue to pull back the protective paper, smoothing the film down onto the vase.*

3 Draw the design onto paper and place this inside the vase. Trace the design through the glass and onto the film, with a felt-tip pen.

4 With a scalpel knife cut around the outline of the pattern.

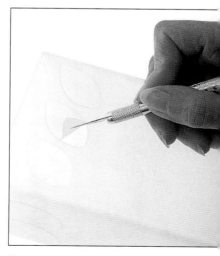

5 Cut and remove the surrounding resist, taking care not to lift off the area of resist on the design. Spend a few moments rubbing the edges of the design so they are firmly in contact with the glass. The force of the sandblaster could lift these pieces if they are not secure.

6 Put the prepared vase in the sandblasting machine and hold with one hand while you blast with the other. When finished, rinse with water.

7 Rinse the pieces of resist with the scalpel and rinse again to remove any glass dust.

LEAF IN THE FALL

You will need

* red on yellow French flashed glass
* straightedge
* glass cutter
* grozier pliers
* vinyl resist
* paper and pencil
* felt-tip pen
* scalpel
* orange stick
* wood adhesive
* brass strip for edging
* flux and brush
* solder and soldering iron
* brass wire for hanging

1 *Following the pattern on page 150, use the straightedge to score the straight lines. Break the glass to the size indicated on the pattern.*

2 *If the break is not completely successful, use the pliers to "nip" off irregular edges.*

3 *Cut a piece of resist larger than the size of the glass.*

4 *Peel back a small section of the protective paper and lay the resist onto the flashed side of the glass.*

5 *As you pull back the paper about 2.5 cm (an inch) at a time, smooth the film down to make firm contact with the glass. Moving too quickly can cause air bubbles.*

6 *Trace the design on the pattern through the glass with a felt-tip pen.*

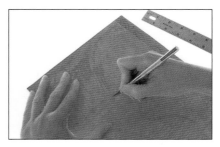

7 *Carefully score the outline of the leaf.*

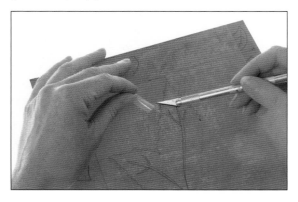

8 *Remove the film from around the leaf but leave the border covered. Cut and pull thin strips of the film away on the inside of the leaf. Cut out the oval leaves on the border and remove the film from these shapes only.*

9 With the orange stick, apply thin lines of detail with wood adhesive on the exposed red glass. Allow to dry. Place the panel into the sandblasting unit with the resist side of the glass facing you. Close the door. The sand jet should be sprayed across the glass surface in a continuous sweeping motion. Depending upon the pressure and the type of abrasive sand (49psi with a fine grit is recommended), the red flash glass will be removed quickly. Start from the top and work downwards taking care to keep the jet moving constantly. Notice how a shading effect can be achieved as the sand removes the flash. When all of the red has been removed, stop blasting and remove the panel from the unit. Peel off all the resist and wash the panel carefully.

10 Mitre some brass edging to fit around the panel.

11 Flux and solder the corners and add two loops of brass wire at each corner for hanging.

SHELL MIRROR

You will need
• • • • • • • • • • • • •

* 3 mm (¹/₈ inch) mirrored glass
* glass cutter
* grozier pliers
* paper, pencil and ruler
* scissors
* scapel
* vinyl resist
* felt-tip pen
* wet and dry sandpaper
* small square block of wood with D ring screwed on
* strong adhesive

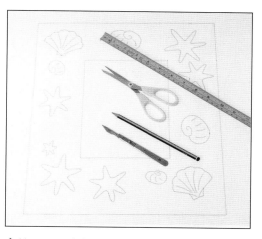

1 *Measure and draw the pattern on page 151 to size. Cut the mirror to size.*

2. *Slowly peel back the protective paper from the resist and apply it to the edge of the mirror. Carefully rub down the adhesive film as you peel back the paper inch by inch.*

3 *Cut the rectangle from the pattern and centre it on the resist-covered mirror.*

4 Mark around it with a felt-tip pen.

5 Cut out the designs from the pattern, arrange them on the border and mark around them with a pen.

6 With a scalpel cut around these shapes. Leave the resist on the rectangle and on the shells and starfish. These will remain reflective.

7 Copy the detail freehand on to the shells.

8 Make sure the resist is firmly in contact with the mirror backing and carefully rub down the resist, especially on the edges.

Prop the mirror into the sandblasting machine with the resist and mirror backing facing you. Close the door and turn on the compressor and extractor. Using pressure of no more than 40 psi, blast the exposed areas, moving the nozzle from left to right and from top to bottom. Blast until all the mirror backing has been removed.

Wash off the sand from the mirror and use the wet and dry sandpaper to smooth the edges. Allow to dry before screwing a picture hook or D ring onto a 7.6-cm square (3-inch square) piece of wood and glue this to the back for hanging.

Using Glass Painting

Glass painting has been used to decorate leaded glass windows throughout the centuries. It is an exacting technique and is very different from many other forms of pictorial painting.

Paint for glass – which is a mixture of metallic oxides in the form of powder – is ground and mixed with water and some gum arabic. Much of the method of painting on glass is not just applying the paint but also removing it to create texture and shading. The finished work is fired in a kiln that fuses the painting to the glass. Rent or borrow space in a kiln at a local studio or art college if you do not have ready access to one.

ABOVE *A Victorian painted roundel depicts a robin on a bramble stem. Set into a traditional leaded panel, it is an excellent example of early domestic stained glass.*

ABOVE *Each section of this leaded panel was copied from a medieval window. The artist used trace and matt paints to achieve these effects.*
Judith Sovin

ABOVE AND BELOW *Two contemporary yet classical leaded panels that incorporate exquisitely painted Victorian glass fragments into the design.*
Leo Amery

ABOVE *An autonomous leaded panel displays a fine example of painting, silver staining and acid etching.*
Judith Sovin

PEAR PANEL

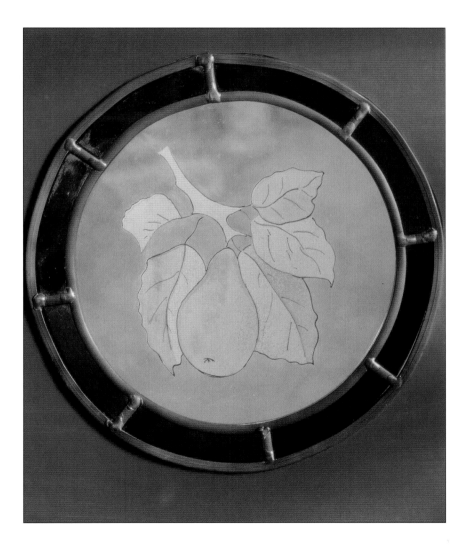

You will need

✳ polish antique clear and dark green glass

for painting:

✳ black trace paint

✳ gum arabic

✳ palette knife

✳ scrap of glass to serve as palette

✳ trace brush

✳ shade paint for matting

✳ mop brush

✳ badger brush

✳ stipple brush

✳ short stiff paintbrush

✳ silver stain

✳ washing-up sponge with abrasive side

for leading:

✳ glass cutter

✳ grozier pliers

✳ horseshoe nails

✳ U section lead

✳ H section lead

✳ tallow candle

✳ solder

✳ soldering iron

This project combines painted glass with leading. It is best to make it with a U lead border as it has been designed as a piece to hang. It is not cemented as other leaded projects because it is not to be used externally. However, there's no reason why it could not be adapted for a window panel if you wish.

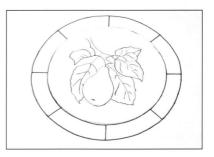

1 *Clean the piece of clear antique glass and place directly over the pattern (taken from page 152) in preparation for painting.*

2 *Mix the trace paint thoroughly after adding a few drops of water to obtain a thick creamy consistency. Add only a few drops at a time.*

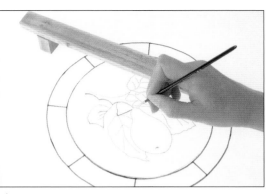

3 *Mix and grind the paint well with the palette knife. Add a drop of gum arabic. Mix again and add some more water to obtain a workable consistency. Test the mixture on a separate piece of glass with a brush to check its density.*

4 *Load the trace brush with paint and, while resting your arm on a rest, make one continuous stroke with the brush. This may require some practice to start with, but if you make a mistake the paint can be wiped off (but this must be done thoroughly) and you can begin again. Remember never to re-touch a stroke or go over a painted line with another, as the paint will blister in the kiln. Each sweep with the brush must be a single movement. Reload the brush and begin the next line just where the previous one ended.*

When the tracing is complete, fire the piece at a temperature of 675°C (1250°F). Care should be taken when removing the glass from the kiln as there is a danger of the piece cracking with a sudden change of temperature. Allow the piece to rest in the kiln after firing is complete until the temperature has dropped below 200°C (395°F). Electric kilns generally have annealing chambers for this purpose.

5 *Mix the shade paint in the same way as the trace paint and apply with sweeps of the mop brush.*

6 *Move the paint over the glass in different directions using the badger brush; be sure to maintain a consistent layer on the surface.*

7 *After the paint has dried, use the stipple brush to dab the paint and create a texture on the surface. Stipple a little more in some areas to achieve lighter tones.*

8 *With the end of a paintbrush or a stick, define the outline. Remove the excess paint with a short stiff paintbrush. Fire the piece once again at approximately 675°C (1250°F). (This will vary with different kilns.)*

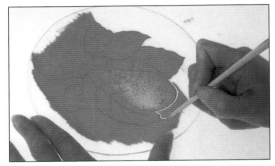

9 *Now mix the silver stain, but it is not necessary to add gum arabic. Apply it to the back of the glass with a mop brush (keep stain brushes separate from shading brushes) and then "sweep" it with light, even strokes in different directions with the badger brush, maintaining a consistent layer. Remove excess paint from around the pear as you would for shade colour. Fire the piece at approximately 600°C (1110°F). When it has been fired and cooled, remove the residue on the back of the glass by washing with the abrasive side of the washing-up sponge.*

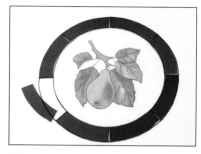

10 *Cut the glass pieces surrounding the painted section and assemble them.*

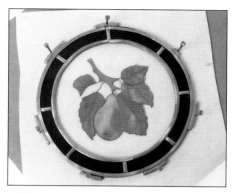

11 *Surround the painted disc in lead first and then add the intersected lead and glass border. The exterior lead is pinned in place with horseshoe nails. Place scrap lead in between the exterior lead and the nails for protection.*

12 *Apply tallow wax to the intersecting joints.*

13 *Now solder the joints. Turn the disc over and apply the wax and solder.*

PAINTED MOON

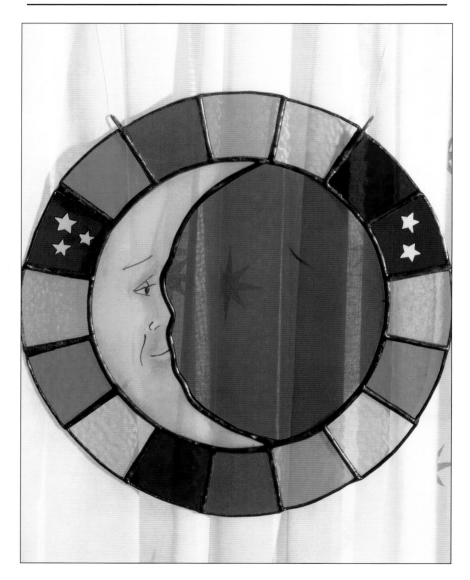

You will need

glass for border:

* ✳ various colours of rolled cathedral and dark blue flash
* ✳ blue antique glass for background
* ✳ yellow antique glass for moon
* ✳ glass cutter
* ✳ grozier pliers
* ✳ carborundum stone
* ✳ 0.8 mm ($^1/_{32}$ inch) copper foil
* ✳ solder and soldering iron
* ✳ flux and flux brush
* ✳ copper sulphate
* ✳ picture wire for hanging

for painting:

* ✳ trace paint
* ✳ shading colour
* ✳ gum arabic
* ✳ glass palette
* ✳ palette knife
* ✳ trace brush
* ✳ mop brush
* ✳ badger brush
* ✳ short-bristle hoghair brush

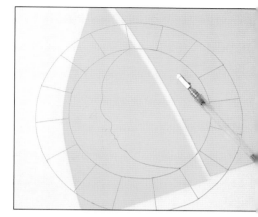

1 *For the moon, score and break a section of glass to a suitable size. Make at least two copies of the pattern on page 153.*

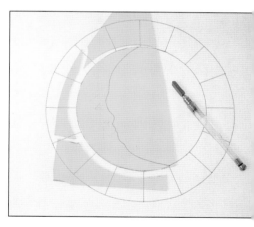

2 *Following the pattern, score the outside curve first and break.*

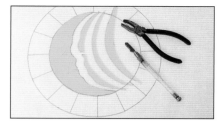

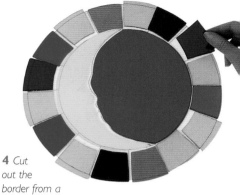

3 Score the inside following the curves of the face. Make a series of scores next to each other and with the pliers, break each one. Hold the pliers next to the score each time. Hold the glass firmly with the other hand. If there is too much resistance when you try to pull out the glass, use the end of a cutter to tap the score from underneath until you see a change in the appearance of the score. Use the pliers to ease the glass out.

4 Cut out the border from a selection of colours. Check that all the pieces fit well on the pattern. Two pieces of the glass we have chosen are flashed and will be sandblasted (see step 8).

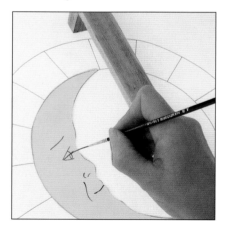

5 To paint the face of the moon, first mix the trace paint and then apply. With the arm on a rest to steady the hand, make one continual stroke with the trace brush for each line on the face. Fire the moon in the kiln at approximately 675°C (1250°F).

6 Mix the shade colour and after applying with a mop brush make some criss-cross or diagonal strokes with the badger to distribute the paint evenly.

7 *We used a short-bristle hoghair paintbrush to stipple the shade colour to tone and contour the face. The moon is fired once again at the same temperature.*

8 *Cover the pieces of blue glass in the border with resist and cut out small star shapes to expose the flashed glass ready for sandblasting. (This technique is optional to the project but is described in the chapter on sandblasting.)*

9 *Carefully rub the edges of all the pieces with the stone, then wash and foil them.*

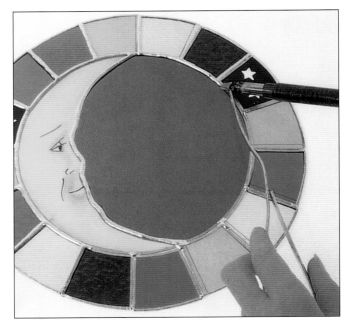

10 *Flux and tack solder the pieces in place. Flux once again and tin solder the whole project both front and back. On the front side only, bead the seam with more solder. To hang the project, two short pieces of copper or brass picture wire can be formed into loops and soldered into the seams. Always solder these into the vertical seam and not just along the top or outside edge of the foil, as they will not hold the weight of the item. Finish with the copper sulphate patina and wash thoroughly.*

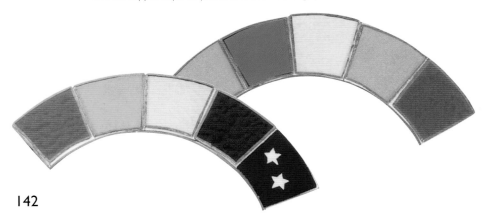

GALLERY

ABOVE AND RIGHT *Leaded and painted window panels commissioned by a literary agent to commemorate her involvement with publishing. Note the graphic use of paint on the leaves and figures.*

ABOVE *Two of these panels have been restored to match the originals. They incorporate painted, stained and enamelled roses.*

143

PATTERNS

Enlarge by 240%

PATTERNS

Enlarge by 190%

PATTERNS

The Tiffany-style lampshade is one of a wide selection of kits available from specialized stained glass suppliers. Here are just four other traditional designs available.

PATTERNS

Enlarge by 200%

PATTERNS

Enlarge to fit
your window

PATTERNS

Here are five various designs which are easy to trace and cut from vinyl resist to apply to your vase ready for sandblasting. Simple shapes, such as these, generally work better than complex shapes for newcomers to this technique.

PATTERNS

Enlarge by 165%

PATTERNS

Enlarge by 240%

PATTERNS

Enlarge by 170%

PATTERNS

Enlarge by 200%

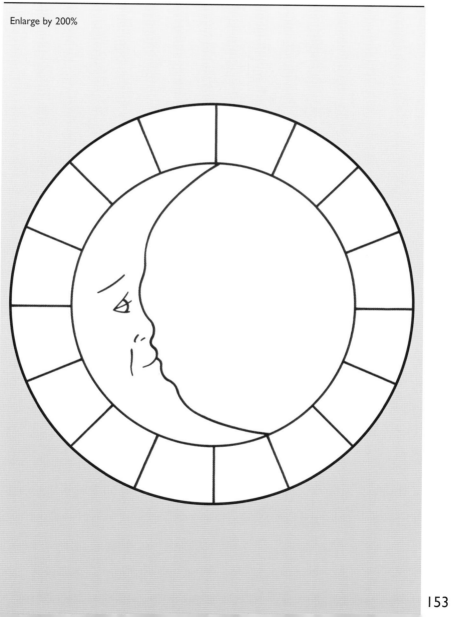

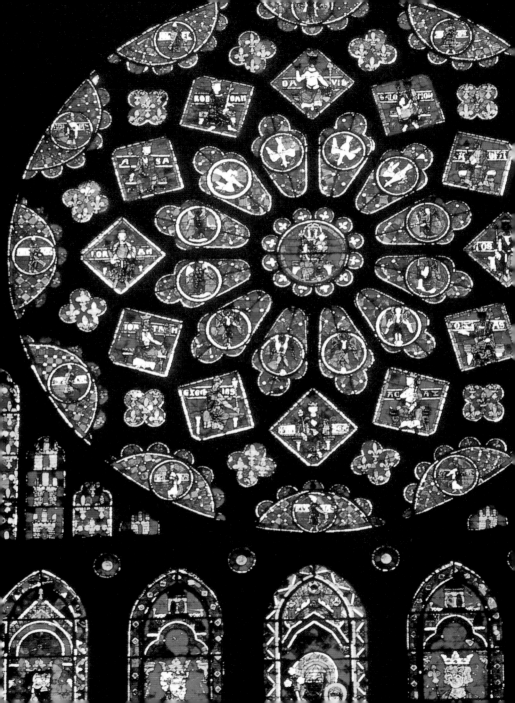

Stained Glass through the Ages

There can be few people who are not
moved as they stand beneath a medieval
stained glass window, gazing at the glowing
colours and intricate pattern, perhaps set
in a delicate web of stone tracery. Sunlight
streaming through lays at their feet the
medieval glazier's art, which has survived
nearly a millennium of war, plague and
iconoclasm. Stained glass is as much a part
of Gothic architecture as soaring vaulted
naves and lavishly carved porches.
The oldest surviving stained glass windows
are preserved in Augsburg Cathedral in
Germany, and are thought to date from
the end of the 11th century. It was,
however, a development in architecture,
rather than art, that nurtured the flowering
of medieval stained glass.

Gothic Architecture

The period of architecture known as Gothic – a derogatory 18th-century reference to the barbaric Goths – had its birth in the 12th century, when Abbé Suger began to rebuild the rich and powerful royal abbey of St. Denis in Paris.

By this time the graceful pointed arch had begun to replace the squat round arch of Romanesque architecture. Previously only small, isolated windows could pierce the walls and thick pillars that supported the weight of the roof. But at St. Denis much of the thrust of the roof vault was carried to the ground independently of the walls by outside buttresses, allowing between them "wonderful and uninterrupted light of the most radiant windows". As luxury and daring were expressed in increasing height, so the buttress projected further out, thus becoming

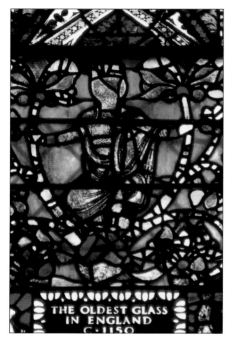

ABOVE *Believed to be the earliest extant stained glass in England, this panel is thought to show a king entwined in the branches of a Jesse Tree.* **York Minster c. 1150.**

the "flying" buttress – the symbol of Gothic architecture.

The Gothic style admirably expressed growing affluence, the power of the Church and the genuine religious zeal of the time. Magnificent cathedrals soared above town roofs, displaying rich carvings and stained glass. Probably the most beautiful as well as the best preserved early Gothic cathedral is at Chartres in France, which was begun at the end of the 12th century after fire had destroyed an earlier church on the site. Its scale, architectural confidence and window glazing influenced building and

stained glass throughout Europe from the 13th century on. The windows remain an inspiration and wonder to the onlooker today, as well as a testament to the skill of the craftsmen who created them.

BELOW *Flying buttresses are a feature of Gothic architectiure and were designed to support some of the weight of the roof vault, allowing larger window spaces.* **Chartres Cathedral.**

ABOVE *The Five Sisters window in York Minster is the finest and largest example of "grisaille" to be found in England. The window is an intricate cobweb of foliage and ornamental patterns.*

Early English Stained Glass

It is difficult to identify the first purely English stained glass. Only a small amount of clear glass was being made at this time, and any coloured glass was imported from the Continent.

ABOVE *The Jordan window in Canterbury Cathedral.*

BELOW *Glimpses of secular life and national and local customs are provided by small roundels or panels depicting the Twelve Labours of the Months. They were usually found in private houses, colleges or guildhalls. This roundel, representing February, shows a figure warming himself by a fireside.* **English, 15th century.**

In 1174, the choir of Canterbury Cathedral was destroyed by fire and, as a result of close Anglo-Norman links at the time, a Norman, William of Sens, was invited to England to help restore the cathedral. He brought with him both stone for rebuilding and coloured glass for the windows. The earliest stained glass in Canterbury appears in the north rose window, which seems to have been completed by 1178. However, an earlier example, thought to date from 1150, can be found at York Minster, on a single remaining panel depicting a king seated in the branches of a Jesse Tree. Gradually the building of great English cathedrals and enlargement of important Saxon churches began to compete with the magnificence of the monastic abbeys, which until then had reigned supreme. Rich stained glass often filled the windows as each building sought to impress its neighbours and worshippers, even in the most humble parish churches.

It was, however, sometimes a matter of controversy whether the so-called "rainbow of light" should or should not fill a church. Ascetics such as Bernard of Clairvaux, founder of the strict Cistercian Order, disapproved of these "coloured gems" and declared

LEFT *Early 13th century window in Canterbury, Kent, depicting Moses' spies returning from the Promised Land.*

that too much ornament in a church distracted men's minds and diverted monks from contemplation. In 1134, the Chapter of the order decreed that only clear glass could be used in the windows of their churches. Following this edict to live "pure and harmonious lives," a grey/green-tinted glass with simple geometric and natural patterns, known as "grisaille," was introduced. Because it was cheaper than coloured glass, it became widely used. A fine example of this work is the Five Sisters window in York Minster, and there is another in the Lady Chapel window at Hereford Cathedral.

Pictures in Glass

Throughout the medieval period, the Church wielded great power over the community. Simple untutored men and women received religious instruction – and sometimes thinly veiled propaganda – through stories depicted in stained glass.

Knowledge, formerly available only in frescoes, mosaics and sculpture, was now imparted through the pictures in the windows. The images were symbolic, not factual; for example, the 12th-century window in Canterbury Cathedral called Adam Delving represents the Garden of Eden as a single etiolated tree.

The stories in the windows were based on events and characters from the Old Testament known as "types," and paralleled those characters and events thought to reappear in the New Testament that were termed "antetypes". For example, Jonah being swallowed by the whale and delivered up after three days prefigures Christ's Entombment and

ABOVE *Ornate 14th-century canopy in Gedney Church, Lincolnshire. The window depicts architectural features and is surrounded by a border of stylized foliage.*

Resurrection. A good series of these windows is at King's College Chapel, Cambridge. The genealogy of Christ was a popular subject, as were stories from The Golden Legend, a book that related the lives and legends of the saints. There was no attempt to present the figures realistically, a practice that mirrored the visual art of the period in tapestry, heraldry and frescoes.

Windows depicting lives and miracles of the saints were used for intercession – and woe betide anyone who, having received a benefit from one of these saints, failed to give the Church gifts in money or kind in

payment. Such saints would be placed in the windows in a stained glass framework or canopy to show their importance. Initially the canopies were simple, but as time passed they followed the architectural style and became very tall and grand. The borders were often made up in grisaille and decorated with lozenges, circles or squares in a geometric pattern, or foliage, and particularly in the 14th century, with tiny heraldic devices, faces or grotesques. Stained glass was expensive and small remaining pieces would be used up in this way to eliminate waste. By the 16th century, the use of a wide border design around the window had dwindled or even disappeared. The figures themselves spread across the design and the canopies were depicted as alcoves with supporting pillars that soared up into pinnacles and occasionally occupied half the window.

Symbolic or iconographic imagery was gathered from the Bible, in those days the Latin Vulgate version. Perhaps the most famous symbol was the Jesse Tree. It represents in picture form the prophecy of Isaiah that the Messiah would descend from Jesse, the father of King David. This royal lineage was depicted by a tree growing from Jesse's loin with Mary as its stem and Christ as its fruit or flower. The earliest example of this iconography can be seen at St. Denis, but the finest Jesse Tree is

generally held to be that in the west wall at Chartres. An interesting example at Dorchester Abbey in Oxfordshire has the stone tracery of the window as the tree and the stained-glass panels as the branches.

Simple portraits of the donor of the window or part of the building first appeared in the representation of Abbé Suger in an apse window in St. Denis. Figures would normally be depicted at the foot of the window, sometimes with wives and children kneeling in supplication or holding out a model of the church or window to the saint to whom it was dedicated.

ABOVE *This window in the Abbey Church of St. Denis in Paris depicts the kneeling figure of Abbé Suger, who had the church rebuilt in 1140.*

Occasionally the figures appeared in tracery lights and their heraldry was shown in the form of simple shields, indicating the name and rank of the donor so that their benevolence might be recognised. Details of costume indicated the status of a donor figure – a king wore a crown, a bishop a mitre. Subsequently, as Eastern influence filtered in via the Crusades and later through trade, the style of dress altered to reflect the times.

Mid- to Late Gothic

By the beginning of the 14th century, it is estimated that some 80 cathedrals and 500 churches of near-cathedral size had been started in France alone, following the consecration of St. Denis.

In England the Early Gothic cathedrals of Lincoln, Wells and Salisbury were built at this time. Later, the style called "Opus Francigenum" – in recognition of its origin – inspired the builders of the great cathedrals of Cologne and Strasbourg in Germany, Sienna in Italy (with its marbled striped façade), and those at Búrgos, Toledo and León in Spain.

As the plague known as the Black Death took its toll, the 14th century saw the population of England reduced by one-third. By this time the Early English Period of architecture had given way to the mid-Gothic Decorated Period. Sadly, much 13th-century glass was removed or broken to make way for the new, freer style, with its tracery and curved shapes. Windows often became larger and the areas of glass between the stone mullions longer and narrower, with tracery above. Small pictures were created across the lights, and stylised designs gave way to more flowing forms.

PAINTING AND STAINING

During this period, as the glaziers vied with each other to create ever more beautiful windows, painting, using oxides of iron fired into the glass, became more naturalistic. The discovery of staining in the early 14th century gave glaziers a completely new palette of yellows – as well as the name of their craft. This technique involved the application of a nitrate of silver to white glass, which, when fired in a kiln, stained the glass yellow. The glass painters were enthusiastic in their use of this new "colour" and introduced it at every possible opportunity. It is thought that one of the windows in the north aisle of the nave of York Minster contains the first use of this technique in English glass painting. One of its advantages was that larger pieces of glass could be used, resulting in fewer lead lines; for instance, a head could also include a crown and halo.

Another technique dating from Romanesque times was the flashing of glass. This involved taking a base of white glass onto which was added a thin layer or "flash" of red glass. This could be abraded away in places, allowing white and red on the same piece of glass. Ruby was the most common colour in this treatment; in some areas the ruby flash could be left, and in others removed to leave the clear glass underneath, which could

ABOVE *This Jesse Tree is believed to be one of the first windows of its kind and the model for many others. It shows the genealogy of Christ and dates from* c. 1140.
Notre-Dame Cathedral, Chartres.

then be yellow stained and painted. By the 16th century blue glass was also treated in this way, allowing heraldic devices to be accurately portrayed in stained glass windows.

LATE GOTHIC

The 15th century was a time of growing prosperity, despite the War of the Roses in England and fighting that racked the Continent. Stained glass was part of a flourishing artistic endeavour that spread across Europe. In England, rich wool and cloth merchants, anxious to secure a place in the afterlife, gave freely towards the cost of windows and the building of bigger churches. Coloured glass, however, was still expensive, even for well-to-do merchants, and as windows in the new perpendicular style became larger, they incorporated more clear glass with increased painting and staining.

Merchants' marks on windows depicting tools or symbols connected with their trade - as well as windows donated by the crafts guilds themselves - give an interesting insight into the ordinary domestic lives of both rich and poor in the Middle Ages. Roundels showing the Twelve Labours of the Months, already popular in northern Europe, were placed in private houses, colleges, guildhalls and occasionally, churches.

The Renaissance

Schools of skilled glass painters emerged at Norwich and York, both with distinctive styles and especially adept at figure painting. Elsewhere, new talent and innovation also appeared.

At Warwick John Prudde, the King's Glazier, included in his stained glass decoration holes drilled in the hems of garments of distinguished figures in which he placed small pieces of coloured glass, creating the effect of jewels. It is interesting that Theophilus, probably writing in the 12th century, had described coloured glass being ground into powder to make a paste, which when fired onto the glass was used as "jewels" to decorate crowns or mitres; this process, however, proved unsatisfactory, as the "jewels" fell off. Later attempts in the 15th century to stick coloured glass onto clear panes to achieve a similar effect were equally unsuccessful.

By the end of the 1400s, the invention of the printing press had meant that woodcuts were widely

RIGHT *To create the decorative border on the male figure's gown, the glazier made holes into which small pieces of coloured glass were inserted.* **Lady Chapel, Evreux, France.**

ABOVE *England's only surviving 12th-century rose window, showing The Law and the Prophets. The central circle dates from 1178 and depicts Moses and a blindfolded figure, symbolizing the Synagogue, holding the symbols of law, surrounded by four women representing the virtues.*
North rose window, Canterbury Cathedral.

landscape scenes, at which Flemish and Swiss artists, in particular, excelled.

Sadly, the influence of the Renaissance masters had a detrimental effect as the glaziers tried to copy the meticulous details of the painting, thus ignoring the lead lines and making a picture on glass instead of a picture from glass. The result was uninspired and heavy, with the glass losing its sparkle and translucency. By the end of the 15th century, the skills that had been acquired over 300 years began to fade.

BELOW *The rose window in Sens Cathedral typifies the flamboyant tracery patterns of the 16th-century Gothic architecture.*

available. This had a very powerful influence on stained glass, as ready-made popular designs, including the works of masters such as Holbein and Dürer, could be reproduced by the painter on stained glass without the involvement of an artist. Painting became much more subtle in colour and shading, and a new flesh tone was achieved by the application of sanguine. The use of enamel paints became increasingly common in the search for realism, and leading, which in earlier work had helped to create a picture with a strong outline, now became less important. Some of the finest painted glass was in the form of small roundels of genre and

The Reformation

The protestant revolutions in northern Europe in the early 16th century resulted in enormous upheaval, with many people fleeing their homes and even their countries.

German and Flemish glaziers emigrated to England and set up workshops at Southwark, where their arrival was bitterly resented by the English glass painters who had practised there since the 13th century. The emigrants' finest work appears in King's College Chapel at Cambridge, which is a watershed in

ABOVE Christ Redeems Souls from Hell, *one of 26 windows in the main chapel of King's College, Cambridge, dating from 1515 to 1530.*

the art of English stained glass. This climax of Renaissance stained glass, commissioned in 1515 and not finished until about 1540, depicts events of the Christian faith, from the Annunciation to the Assumption. To achieve this monumental task, the glaziers adopted a new method, carrying the picture right across the window lights and intervening stone mullions, as though painting a huge canvas. However one may admire the artistic quality of the painted glass, the role of the glazier had been totally subordinated to that of the painter. With the increasing use of paint and, later, enamels, pot-metal glass fell from favour and became scarce. This in turn encouraged more enamel painting, and beautiful mouth-blown coloured glass in windows all but disappeared.

The dissolution of the monasteries by Henry VIII, from 1536 to 1540, caused the destruction of many religious works of art, none suffering as much as stained glass. Whole windows were broken up, and more; in the Lady Chapel in Ely Cathedral, all the beautiful carvings, as well as the glass, were smashed wantonly. The result of this ruination was the loss of much of the country's medieval glass.

17th-Century Enamel Painting

It was not until the destruction in the previous century had abated that a religious revival in the early 1600s allowed the use of stained glass again.

Skills, however, had been largely lost, including that of making coloured glass. Enamelling by painting coloured pigment directly onto the surface of clear glass, together with staining, became common, with rectangular panes being used to fill a window.

ABOVE Tobias and Sarah, *a Flemish stained glass panel, 15th century.*

may be seen in the Oxford colleges of Balliol, Christ Church, Wadham and Lincoln, and also in the east window of Peterhouse College, Cambridge, and at Lydiard Tregoze in Wiltshire. Similar work by Baptista Sutton, an Englishman

Under the patronage of Archbishop William Laud, two exceptional Flemish enamel painters, the brothers Abraham and Bernard van Linge, were invited to England, where they executed a number of richly coloured pictorial and figurative windows. The best of these who was well known during this period, can be seen at the Trinity Chapel of the Abbot's Hospital in Guildford. The increase in stained glass work at this time was such that the London Glaziers' Guild petitioned successfully to become a City Company.

ABOVE *28 late 15th-century windows remain intact in St. Mary's Church, Fairford, Gloucestershire. This panel depicts the Mouth of Hell from the Last Judgement window.*

The revival, however, was short-lived. Following the executions of Charles I and Archbishop Laud, the Cromwellian era brought forth a new outbreak of iconoclasm – and the loss of more glass. In some instances, only crucifixes and faces were vandalized, but there were also instances where the glass was removed and hidden for safety, or even, as at York, preserved in exchange for surrender of the city. One exceptional example that survived was the series of 28 magnificent 15th-century windows at St. Mary's Church in Fairford, Gloucestershire. It was not until after the Restoration of 1660 that religious tolerance returned.

In the latter half of the century, with stained glass skills at a low ebb, heraldic painting came to the fore. Heraldic devices had been used on the Continent as early as the 13th century and appear in stained glass at Chartres. The earliest surviving English examples are in the west window of Salisbury Cathedral. By the end of the 17th century, the leading painter was Henry Gyles of York (1645–1709), whose work was meticulous in detail and extremely elaborate examples are in University College, Oxford, and Acomb, North Yorkshire, where Charles II's coat of arms may be seen. In North America the Dutchman Everett Duycking, who settled in New Amsterdam – now New York – in the mid-17th century, was paid in furs for his heraldic painting on glass.

LEFT *Enamel-painted 18th-century window depicting the Baptism in the River Jordan, designed by Francisco Slater and painted by Joshua Price.* Church of St. Michael and All Angels, Great Witley, Worcestershire.

The 18th Century

During the 1700s, the Price family carried on this tradition of heraldic work in England.

The brothers William and Joshua and the latter's son, William, followed the techniques initiated by the van Linges. It is thought that Joshua was the most gifted of the family, and his enamel painting on a series of windows in Great Witley Church, in Worcestershire, is a fine example of his work. The west window of Westminster Abbey was painted by William Price the Younger in 1735; other examples by the family are the rose window in the north transept of Westminster Abbey and fine windows on the south side of New College Chapel, Oxford.

Towards the end of the century there was little interest in stained glass, and what remained often suffered from lack of repair and unsympathetic restoration. However, connoisseurs such as William Jerningham and Horace Walpole began to study and

collect antiquities, including stained glass (though others, such as James Wyatt, regarded it as 'barbaric'). This flicker of interest was to become a flame of extraordinary brightness in the next century. Meanwhile, across the channel in France, the Revolution was destroying a wealth of medieval and later glass, though Chartres Cathedral was to be spared the destruction.

ABOVE *Detail of The Flight into Egypt, designed by Edward Burne-Jones for Morris & Co, 1862.*
St. Michael's Church, Brighton, E Sussex.

The Victorian Era

The 19th century spanned an era of immense social, political and industrial change, both in Europe and North America.

Architecture and art reflected the aspirations, technical innovation and growing wealth of the industrial nations. Style and fashion, too, spread by improving communications, increasingly influenced the arts and for the first time allowed a national and later an international market. To satisfy demand, industry and art turned to each other, passing from almost total independence at the beginning of the century to fashion-conscious interdependence at the end. Stained glass was no exception in this industrial and artistic revolution.

The previous century's use of colour on, rather than in, glass continued in the early years. Stained glass was the skill of the painter, filling his glass canvas with a picture that ignored glazing bars and used the building structure as its frame. What now displaced this was a return to the skill of the medieval craftsman and the rediscovery of the beauty of glass itself. It was this going back to the fundamentals of stained glass that enabled the

revival of the early part of the century to blossom into a thriving craft industry, eventually employing hundreds of workers.

ABOVE *Christ in Glory by Michael O'Connor, 1871, reveals the designer's distinctive geometric style in the canopies.* **St. Andrew's Church, Trent, Dorset**

The Gothic Revival

The origins of this reappraisal lay in the previous century, when a study of history and archaeology, and an appreciation of the arts, became fashionable.

Grand Tours to the Continent by the wealthy produced an interest in classical art and medieval history and the collections of art resulting from these tours were displayed, discussed and written about. Thus, what had started as a hobby became an influence – and grew into a style. Foremost among these great collectors was Horace Walpole (1717–97), son of the great Whig Prime Minister of England, whose house outside London, called Strawberry Hill, exemplified the Gothic Revival. Among Walpole's vast art collection were examples of painted Flemish and other glass, which excited the interest of many of his visitors. These included the leaders and creators of fashion of the time, such as the architect Augustus Welby Pugin (1812–52).

Pugin was the son of a French architect who had fled to England to escape the French Revolution in 1798. He followed his father's profession and later became the foremost architect of his day in England, taking a leading role in establishing the Gothic Revival both in theory and in practice, with a devotional approach spurred on by his conversion to Roman Catholicism at the age of 21. His first church, St.

Mary's in Derby, coincided with Victoria's accession to the throne in 1837, and a fruitful partnership with Sir Charles Barry resulted in his work in the rebuilding of the Houses of Parliament. He successfully developed the early principles of stained glass in spirit as well as design, making much use of it in his own home in Ramsgate. Pugin was a perfectionist, however, and was unable to find a glass painter whom he believed had the necessary sympathy to interpret his designs. He eventually turned to John Hardman, whose studio was to grow into one of the biggest in the country, remaining in family ownership until 1959.

BELOW *Designed by Augustus Pugin and made by William Warrington in 1838, this window depicts the Virgin and child.*
St. Mary's College chapel (RC), Oscott, Sutton Coldfield, Warwickshire

The First Half of the 19th Century

The foremost English stained-glass designer in the early part of the 19th century was Thomas Willement, who was later to have the grand title of Heraldic Artist to King George IV and Artist in Stained Glass to Queen Victoria.

He pioneered the breakaway from the contemporary picture-painting school of glass artists, taking his inspiration from the medieval glaziers. The work carried out by the Shropshire firm of Betton & Evans on the windows of Winchester College provided him with useful knowledge of early stained glass. He made his first window in 1812, and although initially his work was fairly crude, he soon developed a style reminiscent of medieval glass. A typical Willement window contained vignettes of biblical scenes surrounded by borders of foliage or geometric designs. Some of his finest work was in heraldic stained glass, of which the best known is probably the great memorial window at Hampton Court. Two of Willement's

ABOVE *The Flight into Egypt by William Wailes, 1864.* **All Saints Church, Boyne Hill, Berkshire.**

pupils, William Warrington and Michael O'Connor, both worked in the new Gothic Revival style, and carried out several commissions from Pugin's designs in his churches. Pugin also employed William Wales of Newcastle to make some of his windows.

The man who made one of the greatest contributions to the revival of stained glass was neither a stained glass artist nor a craftsman. There had been several unsuccessful experiments seeking to manufacture glass similar to the strongly coloured glass used by medieval glaziers. In the late 1840s Charles Winston, barrister, antiquarian and connoisseur, determined to rediscover the secrets of making pot-metal glass, having been inspired at the age of 18 to design and execute a stained glass window for his father's church at Faringham. Helped by a Dr. Medlock of the Royal College of Chemistry, he discovered that, for instance, the main constituent of blue glass was cobalt – not lapis lazuli as had been previously thought. Similarly, other pieces of early glass were analyzed with the help of chemists employed by the firm of James Powell of Whitefriars.

Around this time, William Edward Chance, a Birmingham glass manufacturer, was also experimenting; eventually, after many years of devoted work, he succeeded in producing glass of a superior quality. As a result of these successful experiments, it again became possible to make the best pot-metal glass (known as "antique" because of its medieval origins), with much of it produced by James Powell & Sons at their Whitefriars Glass Works and Chance Brothers at Smethwick.

LEFT AND ABOVE *The Flight into Egypt by William Wailes, 1864.*
All Saints Church, Boyne Hill, Berkshire.

173

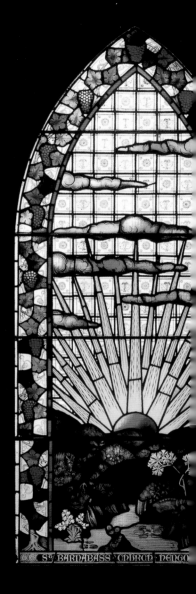

Famous Stained Glass Studios

In the middle of the century, with the support of the influential Cambridge Camden Society and the rise of Anglo-Catholicism, the Victorian imagination was freed and the Gothic style dominated architecture and stained glass in England. This newfound enthusiasm, combined with evangelical fervour in religion, resulted in an enormous surge in the number of churches being built, as well as the "Gothicization" of existing ones. This latter practice was spurred on by the Camden Society, which wanted to rid churches of different architectural styles. In the second half of the century, Victorian ecclesiastical stained glass moved on from its origins in Gothic Revivalism, and developed into a style of its own.

Famous Stained Glass Studios

Stained glass production boomed during the reign of Queen Victoria in the nineteenth century, making this a key period in the history and development of the art form.

Of course, styles varied and fashions changed, and with work rarely signed, or even recorded, the more than 80,000 stained glass windows produced during Victoria's reign can be a bewildering maze for anyone but the expert.

However, some studios rose above the rest in quality and sheer artistry. Among them were Clayton & Bell, which became one of the largest; Heaton Butler & Bayne; Lavers Barraud & Westlake; and later, in the 1870s, Burlison & Grylls. The Gibbs family and

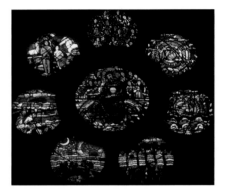

Henry Holiday, many of whose early designs were carried out by the famous firm of James Powell & Sons, also had well-known studios. Their work enriched the Victorian churches of England, the makers usually going unrecognised – except perhaps for the rare symbol or even rarer name – and they remain today a delight to be discovered and enjoyed.

ABOVE *The east rose window in Waltham Abbey, Essex, is an early work by Edward Burne-Jones for James Powell & Sons, 1861.*

LEFT *Queen Victoria Golden Jubilee window by Heaton Butler & Bayne, 1887.* **Great Barton Church, Suffolk.**

CLAYTON & BELL

The partnership of J.R. Clayton and Alfred Bell was formed while they were both working in the large architectural practice of Gilbert Scott. There they also formed a friendship with the architects G.F. Bodley and G.E. Street, who were later to give them important commissions. Their first windows, designed together, were for the nave clerestory in Westminster Abbey and were probably made by the London studio of either Lavers & Barraud or Ward & Hughes. Later they teamed up for a few years with Heaton & Butler, who executed their designs (afterward the latter were joined by Robert Bayne, probably a pupil of Clayton & Bell, to form their own company). One of their most successful commissions, for the church of St. Mary the Virgin at Hanley Castle, Worcestershire, was given to them by Street in 1860. The west window of the Last Judgement is an outstanding example of Clayton & Bell's artistic skill in design and use of colour, and is amongst the best stained glass produced in this period.

Commissions were soon flooding in,

ABOVE *The Last Judgement by Clayton & Bell.*

St. Mary's Church, Hanley Castle, Worcestershire, 1860.

and Clayton & Bell moved to large new premises in London's Regent Street, where they eventually employed about 300 people in their studio. They became one of the most successful stained glass studios in the second half of the century and carried out commissions for the Queen, for which they received the Royal Warrant. Their work can be found all over England, gracing great cathedrals as well as small parish churches. Two of their most notable accomplishments were the large west window of King's College Chapel, Cambridge, and the east window of Bath Abbey. Their work is also in the United States, and includes the window of St. Paul Preaching on Mars Hill, in New York's Church of the Incarnation on Madison Avenue and 35th Street. Almost inevitably the freshness and vitality of Clayton & Bell's earlier work suffered from the enormous output demanded of them, and their later windows can be heavy and stereotyped. By the time of Bell's death in 1895, the firm was being run by their sons. Michael Farrar-Bell, Alfred Bell's descendant, continues his family's tradition to this day.

CHARLES EAMER KEMPE

Another large and famous studio that carried the medieval tradition of stained glass into the 20th century was that of a gifted and deeply religious man, Charles Eamer Kempe. He was born the fifth son of wealthy parents (who gave their name to the Kemp Town development in Brighton), and his main ambition when at Pembroke College, Oxford, was to become a clergyman. This aim was thwarted by a serious speech defect, however, leaving him to pursue his great talent in church decoration and stained glass. He studied under the great neo-Gothic architect G.F. Bodley and later became a student with the firm of Clayton & Bell.

As a child, Kempe was supposed to have had a mystical experience in Gloucester Cathedral, induced by the setting sun casting its light through the windows, and this was said to have strengthened his resolve to work with stained glass in later life. His earliest recorded window, in fact, is Gloucester Cathedral's Bishop Hooper Memorial Window, made by Clayton & Bell in 1865. By 1866, Kempe had set up as an independent designer with two assistants, in a studio that he opened at his London home. Already considered an authority on medieval stained glass, Kempe was consulted on the restoration of the ancient glass at Fairford Church near Cirencester and Nettlestead Church in Kent.

Fifteenth-century stained glass was to inspire Kempe's style and influence all his ecclesiastical stained glass work. His use of blue, green and ruby glass and large areas of silver staining, combined with the delicate and detailed painting of the figures, was a hallmark of his style. His popularity grew, and by the end of the century he was employing more than 50 people. He completed 3,141 commissions for stained glass in Britain and abroad, particularly in the United States, where his glass can be seen in New Haven, Connecticut, in Philadelphia, and in the National Cathedral in Washington, D.C. One of his largest and most successful commissions in England was for Winchester Cathedral.

In spite of a certain amount of repetition of early designs in his later work, occasioned by great success and demand, Kempe never allowed the quality or individuality of his work to deteriorate. His work can often be recognised by the characteristic soft colouring, the exacting draftsmanship, the angels' wings 'colored like peacock feathers', and, after 1895, by the use of a wheatsheaf symbol – taken from his family arms – to sign his work. At the end of the century, when other artists were taking up a new, freer style, Kempe remained loyal to the classic Victorian tradition, which the firm carried on even after his sudden death in London in 1907. He bequeathed the company to his cousin Walter Ernest Tower who, together with four of Kempe's previous colleagues, continued it as a limited company, signing their work with a tower incorporated in the wheatsheaf symbol. His most famous student was Ninian Comper and he, with others, continued Kempe's traditional approach to stained glass, even after the Second World War.

RIGHT *Window designed by C.E. Kempe for Thomas Baillie & Co, 1868.*
St. Mark's Church, Stapleford, Sussex

BELOW *This early four-light window by C.E. Kempe shows use of silver stain to great effect, 1876.*
St. John the Evangelist, High Cross, Hertfordshire.

THE PRE-RAPHAELITES

The Pre-Raphaelite Brotherhood, founded in 1848 by, amongst others, William Holman Hunt, John Everett Millais and Dante Gabriel Rossetti, was an important painterly adjunct to the Gothic Revival. Employing new colouring and bold flowing line to emphasise and enhance designs, they rejected what they considered to be the illusionary idealism of Raphael. The art critic John Ruskin declared, 'Pre-Raphaelitism has but one principle, that of uncompromising truth in all that it does, obtained by working everything down to the most minute detail from nature only' – a belief that truth was to be found in scrupulous attention to fact.

The growing influence of this group affected both art and stained glass as well as the critics and, in turn, the public. However, the man who

dominated not only stained glass but all the applied arts through the latter half of the century – and beyond – was William Morris.

ABOVE *Window designed by Dante Gabriel Rossetti for Morris and Co., 1862, and adapted from a design for the east window in Bradford Cathedral, Manningham Church, Bradford, Yorkshire.*

LEFT *Vyner Memorial window in Christ Church Cathedral, Oxford, by Edward Burne-Jones, 1871. The window commemorates the death of four undergraduates in Greece.*

WILLIAM MORRIS

William Morris's influence in the arts and crafts of the second half of the century is almost incalculable. He was, like Kempe, the son of wealthy parents. After leaving Oxford University, where he began his friendship with Edward Burne-Jones, he was able to indulge his belief in the importance of the individual's contribution in an age of growing mass production. His workshop was founded in 1861 and set up as a craftsmen's cooperative, advocating a return to the high standards of the past in craft and design.

Joined by Burne-Jones, Rossetti, Ford Madox Brown, Philip Webb, Charles Faulkner and P.P. Marshall, Morris started the firm of Morris, Marshall, Faulkner & Company; the only money in hand being £1 from each partner, a contribution from Morris's mother, and a further small amount of cash from each of them. Their aim was to achieve beauty in all things, declaring 'the aim of art is to increase the happiness of men . . .', and they became a close-knit band of artists. Some of their work was displayed in London's second Great International Exhibition of 1862 and, with growing publicity and recognition, they prospered, eventually moving to larger premises with more staff, including apprentices recruited from the boys' homes in Euston Road, London.

In contrast to other stained glass work at that time, they adopted a free-flowing style in both lead lines and painting with strong vibrant colours and naturalistic form. Burne-Jones was the artist who put the firm's ideas into designs and cartoons: one of his most successful windows is that of the Kingdom of Heaven in St. Michael and All Angels, Lyndhurst, Hampshire, 1862–63. As well as ecclesiastical work, they carried out many domestic commissions, some as part of their wide-ranging decorative skills that encompassed textile and wallpaper production, furniture making and printing.

THE AESTHETIC MOVEMENT

Morris's ideals were taken up by others, who, while perhaps not sharing his socialist principles, reacted against High Victorian taste in the traditional treatment of stained glass. They believed in a decorative art in harmony with the surrounding architecture, taking its inspiration from nature and natural form. Their figures were full of movement and grace, with backgrounds of leaves and plants. Stained glass in hall windows, borders to doors, and fanlights became fashionable, and opened up new markets. The standard of work was generally high and the designs original, although even Burne-Jones could often only meet demand by adapting previously successful work; his figure of St. Martin, designed for the east window of St. Martin, Brampton, Cumberland, in 1880, was thought to have been repeated at least 40 times between 1883 and 1935.

One of the most significant stained glass artists at this time was Henry Holiday. He rejected sheer imitation of the Gothic style and instead took his

RIGHT
Window designed by Henry Holiday for Lavers & Barraud, 1865.
Worcester College, Oxford.

ABOVE *The Angel Musician by Edward Burne-Jones for Morris & Co., 1882, is very rich in colour and punctuated with decorative stars.*
St. Peter and St. Paul, Cattistock, Dorset.

inspiration from Classical and Renaissance art. Much of his work was executed by James Powell & Sons, although in 1891 he set up his own workshop. His circle included Harry Ellis Wooldridge and Carl Almquist, a Swede who later became chief designer for the Lancaster firm of Shrigley & Hunt. They and their followers of the years 1870 to 1885 are included among the adherents of the so-called Aesthetic Movement, and their stained glass is generally recognisable by its use of muted colour and classical figures. Good examples of their work are Holiday's windows of 1869 in St. Mary Magdalene, Paddington, and Wooldridge's chancel windows at All Saints, West Bromwich, Staffordshire, executed in 1873. In Scotland and the north of England the work of the stained glass artist

Daniel Cottier became extremely popular; in 1873, he opened studios in New York and Sydney, thus spreading the contemporary style of British stained glass and finding a close affinity with Tiffany and La Farge.

SOUTHERN GERMANY AND FRANCE

King Ludwig I of Bulgaria, an eccentric patron of the arts, founded the Munich workshop of the Royal Bavarian Glass Painting Studio in 1827. It was at the centre of the 19th-century revival of stained glass in Germany, and, largely influenced by Italian art, produced predominantly biblical work of indifferent quality. The workshop's heavily enamelled glass, rich and ebullient in the Baroque and Rococo styles, was exported to the United States and some European countries including Scotland, where its windows for Glasgow Cathedral, although in the 19th-century Gothic style, were widely deprecated. The studio continued, however, to enjoy considerable success and appreciation in Germany, where much of its stained glass was lost in the two world wars.

In the 1840s, there was a growing popularity for a group of young German painters who worked in a deserted monastery in Rome and became known as the Nazarenes. They copied such masters as Raphael, Dürer and Perugino, and their "brotherhood" relationship anticipated the English Pre-Raphaelites. Prints of their work were popular with stained glass artists and remained fashionable in Germany until the end of the century.

In France, Eugène-Emanuel Viollet-le-Duc believed, like many of his contemporaries, that colour in glass should replace the duller enamel painting then fashionable. As the Inspector of the Service des Monuments Historiques under Napoleon III, he was responsible for the maintenance and restoration of stained glass windows throughout France, and was therefore in an excellent position not only to influence style in stained glass, but also to do something about his belief. He allied himself with the so-called "Scientific Romantics", who were pledged to revive stained glass in its pure early Gothic form; as a result of their activities, much restoration of old glass was carried out and many new workshops opened. Work came from all over Europe, and when, in the 1850s, the Roman Catholic Archdiocese of New York began building a new cathedral, the commission for the stained glass was given to Henry Ely of Nantes and Nicholas Lorin of Chartres.

Another Frenchman, Eugène Stanislas Oudinot, also carried out commissions for American churches; his window, The Supper at Emmanus, is in

Christ Episcopal Church in the Bronx. Although the Gothic Revival was slow to be embraced in France, with many people still favouring enamelling in the neoclassical or Baroque style, the stained glass at the Paris Exposition Universelle of 1855 encouraged its development and led to wide acceptance of its use, particularly in secular buildings. By the end of the century, stained glass in the new Art Nouveau style was appearing in shops, cafés and office buildings.

EARLY AMERICAN STAINED GLASS

The few glaziers among the very early American colourists had neither the materials nor the skills for making stained glass windows, and it is unlikely that anyone could have afforded to commission them. The very few immigrants who were stained glass artists, most of them from England, brought with them the traditions and fashions of Europe; only later was there a truly American school of stained glass. The great turning point was the introduction of opalescent glass in 1870, when American ideas began to flow to Europe.

One of the earliest names in American stained glass work is that of Richard Upjohn, who was the architect of and, it is believed, designer of the windows for, Trinity Church, at Broadway and Wall Street, Manhattan (1844–45). However, very little indigenous stained glass was produced until after the middle of the century, when William Jay Bolton, son of a wealthy family who emigrated to the United States from England in 1836, came to the fore. His first stained glass window was for his family church in Pelham Bay in New York State's Westchester County, which was followed by numerous commissions, including 60 windows for the Church of St. Ann and the Holy Trinity in Brooklyn Heights, New York. These, along with the windows at Trinity Church, are thought to be the earliest surviving stained glass windows in the country in situ. The oldest stained-glass studio is the firm of J & R Lamb, founded in New York City in 1857 by the English-educated Joseph Lamb, who was assisted by his brother Richard. The firm's tradition is now carried on by Lamb's grandson, Frederick.

RIGHT
Window by Charles Clutterbuck.
St. Michael's Church, Aylsham, Norfolk, c. 1855–57

LEFT AND RIGHT *Window produced by Tiffany Studios at their Corona glassworks on Long Island, entitled Reading of the Scrolls.*

OPALESCENT GLASS

In 1865, a young American artist named Louis Comfort Tiffany crossed the Atlantic to Europe. In France he became fascinated by the richly coloured medieval windows in Chartres Cathedral, and when he compared these with the new stained glass being produced at that time, he found much of the modern glass dull and lifeless, the more so when it was heavily painted. Back in New York in the early 1870s, he began to experiment, seeking to re-create the quality of medieval glass. He noted in a letter that 'I perceived that glass used for claret bottles and preserve jars was richer, finer and had a more beautiful quality than any glass I could buy. So I set to puzzling out this curious matter and found that the glass from which bottles are made contained the oxides of iron and other impurities, which are left in the sand when melted'.

In 1878, Tiffany founded his own glassworks, but after a fire, continued his experiments at the Heide Glasshouse in Brooklyn, where he found John La Farge carrying out similar work. It is likley that both artists compared notes while experimenting with this new material, but there is no evidence of any collaboration between the two. This new glass that they were both striving to develop was called "Favrile", from the Latin for fabricated. Favrile glass was streaked with hues of its own and other colours; the colour was strong and the variety endless, often iridescent and of a milky, opalescent appearance.

It was, in fact, La Farge who obtained the first patent for this revolutionary new glass, in February, 1880, with Tiffany obtaining two patents for variations on the same opalescent glassmaking techniques in November of the same year. The copyright battle for this new material resulted in a great deal of animosity between the two.

Into a New Century

The Arts and Crafts Movement arose from the celebrated art critic John Ruskin's enthusiasm for crafts and craftsmen – the creative workman unhindered by uniformity or mass production and striving for both utility in purpose and beauty in design. The artist/craftsman was the ideal, implementing or at least supervising the work throughout each stage, promoting individualism and rejecting the encroachment of mass production in manufacture. Ruskin's ideals, taken up and so passionately expressed by Morris and his followers, were the intellectual beginnings of a movement that encompassed not only stained glass but other crafts such as textiles, pottery, furniture making and printing.

Into a New Century

The Century Guild, formed in 1882 by A.H. Mackmurdo, was, although short-lived, one of the earliest guilds of the Arts and Crafts Movement.

Two years later, in March 1884, the Art Workers' Guild was founded by students of the famous architect Richard Norman Shaw, who saw their work as art more than a professional process bound by convention and formality. Their motto was 'the unity of the arts', and they welcomed fellow-thinking artists and craftsmen.

The first Arts and Crafts Exhibition, held in London in 1888, proved a great success and subsequent exhibitions followed. By the 1890s, enthusiasm for the movement was apparent in the many small workshops – some grandly calling themselves "Guilds" – that catered to the growing demand for Arts and Crafts products in the home, and as architectural decoration. The art colleges took up the new fashion as well, and their teaching served to influence a new generation. In the United States and Europe, similar ideals and movements sprang up as a result of their national social reactions to mass production. The Arts and Crafts ideal reached its peak in the early years of this century and it was not until the Second World War that it finally lost its appeal.

Of the two main styles of Arts and Crafts stained glass, one was the striking "new" look achieved by the use of slab glass and unusual, often abstract, designs using brilliant colour; the other was the more pictorial and traditional stained glass much in demand, known as "Kempe" style (after Charles Eamer Kempe), which continued to be popular in England and the United

ABOVE *This detail of a five-light window, Christopher Whall's first commission, depicts St. Michael and Eve, 1890–91 Lady Chapel,* **St. Mary's Church, Stamford, Lincolnshire.**

States until the 1930s. Typical of the Arts and Crafts style was the use of more lifelike figures in the windows, in marked contrast to the stiff Victorian forms. Several of the artists could be identified by certain characteristics, for example, Louis Davis always designed beautiful angelic figures in swirling drapery with jewel-like colours and sinuous lead lines, while Selwyn Image's work could be identified by his distinctive style of leading.

PRIOR'S EARLY ENGLISH SLAB GLASS

The Arts and Crafts studios also sought to use only the finest glass, so that in 1888, when a new type of glass was developed that combined bright colour with subtle beauty, they quickly recognised its revolutionary effect. This glass, known as "Prior's Early English" and made in Southwark by Britten & Gilson, was a thick, heavy and unevenly textured blown glass, quite unlike the thinner sheets of "antique" glass. It was made by blowing the molten glass into a box-shaped mould; when cold, the glass was turned out and cut into four rectangular slabs that were thicker at the centre than around the edges, thereby creating denser colour in the middle. With this new glass, lead lines became an important part of the composition. Likewise, the use of intense, vibrant colours, such as

purples, blues, "gold-pink" and emerald, became a hallmark of Arts and Crafts stained glass. A high percentage of white glass was also used; it had a streaky appearance that, combined with matted painting, toned down the intensity of the light and enhanced the iridescent colouring within the glass itself.

CHRISTOPHER WHALL AND HIS CIRCLE

Christopher Whall, who led the Arts and Crafts Movement in stained glass, initially took up painting. He found his career as an artist unsuccessful, however, and in the 1880s, turned to making stained glass. Eventually he set up as an independent designer, greatly influencing his contemporary craftsmen who were reacting against High Victorian taste.

Mary Lowndes, a follower of Whall and one of the earliest female stained-glass artists, took the opportunity of collaborating with the Southwark glass manufacturing firm of Britten & Gilson, which offered stained glass artists the opportunity to work on their own commissions on their factory premises. With Alfred Drury, another gifted artist/craftsman, she founded the firm of Lowndes & Drury. In 1906, they moved to The Glass House at Lettice Street in Fulham, London; this became a popular "open house studio", where artists could work in a fully staffed stained glass workshop, supervising every stage of their work – a process very much in line with the ideals of the Arts and Crafts Movement. Mary Lowndes herself made at least 100 windows, occasionally working with other artists, such as Isabel Gloag.

In Ireland in 1903, another female stained glass artist, Sarah Purser, founded a similar workshop in Dublin, An Túr Gloine (the Tower of Glass), with Alfred Child, a pupil of Whall's, as manager. These studios were central to the development of stained glass in Ireland and were to employ such talented artists as Evie Hone, Harry Clarke, Wilhemina Geddes and Michael Healy. The women took an equal place with the men in the creation of stained glass windows, and equally sought opportunities within the Arts and Crafts Movement for the exchange of ideas with the same idealistic goal, that of harnessing and manipulating light to beautify and enhance their creations.

BELOW *The central figure of St. Francis is surrounded by figures in the Arts and Crafts tradition, by Wilhelmina Geddes, 1930.* **Parish Church, Northchapel, Sussex.**

ABOVE *Detail of window by Mary Lowndes and Isabel Gloag, 1901.* **St. Mary's Church, Slough, Buckinghamshire.**

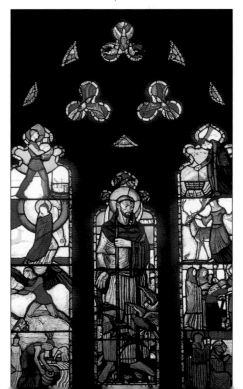

TIFFANY

While the Arts and Crafts Movement in England and Europe was influencing new stained glass there, the work of Louis Comfort Tiffany had begun to excite the fashionable and influential in the United States, where his father's shop in New York was already well known for its jewellery and silverware designs. Using his own opalescent glass, and working with his friend Samuel Colman, Tiffany's first company – called Louis C. Tiffany and Associated Artists – undertook a number of important commissions in New York, including the Seventh Regiment Armory on Park Avenue and the Union League Club (now demolished) on Fifth Avenue and 39th Street. In conjunction with John La Farge, with whom he was later to quarrel, he decorated his own house on East 26th Street. Tiffany's stained glass caused a sensation, and soon he was winning commissions to decorate the houses of the rich and famous. The height of his own success came with a commission from President Chester A. Arthur to decorate the White House; much of his opalescent glass was used, including a large screen of brightly coloured panels featuring national emblems (later, sadly, the screen was destroyed).

In 1885, he renamed his business the Tiffany Glass Company, and his style became fashionable all over the country. His fame spread to Europe as well, and in France he found an admirer and friend in Samuel Bing. Bing was an important supporter of a new movement in the arts in Paris called the Nabis. Like the Arts and Crafts Movement in Britain, the Nabis' ideals spread and they began to influence art and decoration. The first result of collaboration between Tiffany and Bing was a window called The Four Seasons, exhibited in Paris in 1892 and later in London. This work, with its strong and separated colours, its use of small jewel-like pieces of glass, and its free-flowing design, was pure decoration and delighted all those seeking to find a "new art".

BELOW *Tiffany stained glass window, one of three designed for the Red Cross headquarters in Washington, D.C.*

ABOVE *St. Cecelia by Evie Hone, 1950.*
Lanercost Priory, Cumbria

ABOVE *The Adoration of the Magi by Harry Clarke.*
Ashdown Park, Sussex.

ABOVE *Window produced by George Hedgeland from a design by Frank Howard, 1853.* St. Matthew's Church, Ipswich, Suffolk.

ABOVE LEFT AND LEFT *Window designed by Selwyn Image, 1881, for a private house in Mortehoe, Devon.*

ART NOUVEAU

In 1895, Bing opened a shop in Paris, calling it La Maison de l'Art Nouveau. Among the many furnishings and decorative objects sold in the shop was stained glass, including Tiffany's distinctive lamps and Favrile glass objects. The windows in the shop were made by Tiffany to designs by followers of the Nabis, including Pierre Bonnard, Edouard Vuillard and Ker-Xavier Roussel, and set a style that was to take its name from Bing's shop; sadly, these windows are now lost. The Art Nouveau style of stained glass is characterised by its swirling asymmetrical naturalism; clean, sinuous lines often ending in a whiplash; graceful, sensuous female figures, and exaggerated floral and other organic themes. It was considered to have reached its peak at the Exposition Universelle in Paris in 1900, and – although instantly recognisable – Art Nouveau had no strict definition and was more a visual language than a formal statement of design.

In England, Arthur Lasenby Liberty promoted the Art Nouveau style. Associated with Tiffany since the opening of his shop in London's Regent Street in 1875 – and not far from Tiffany & Co's own shop in the same street – Liberty's customers soon included the fashionable decorators of the period, and the style quickly spread. One of Tiffany's most successful but little-known commissions in Great Britain is in the Kirk at Fyvie in Scotland; the window depicts a hauntingly beautiful, young St. Michael, and was designed in memory of Percy Forbes-Leith, a young army officer who had died in South Africa in 1900.

Tiffany's work in the United States started to decrease after the early years of this century, and his decline in popularity was accelerated by the First World War. His control of the firm and its high standards began to slip and by 1928, when Tiffany retired from the company, his style was unfashionable, his work regarded as gaudy and dated. This change in taste caused tragic loss of his glass, as it began to be consigned to attics and, worse, rubbish bins. However, the wheel of fashion has again turned full circle, and now Tiffany's work is much admired. Particularly fine examples of his glass are a two-panel window of exotic birds on a balustrade, commissioned by Capt Joseph R. Delamar and now in Glen Cove, Long Island; a memorial window in the Christ Episcopal Church, Rye, New York, and the collections in The Metropolitan Museum of Art and the Museum of Modern Art in New York City. There are also extensive collections of Tiffany's work in the Corning Museum of Glass, the Charles Hosmer Morse Foundation in Florida, and in the Haworth Art Gallery in Lancashire.

LEFT *Boer War memorial window by Louis C. Tiffany, 1900. The water bottle at David's side is made from the "bull" or eye of a piece of crown-yellow glass.* **St. Cuthbert's Church, Edinburgh.**

ABOVE AND BELOW *Two beautiful Japanese-inspired Art Nouveau panels by William Stewart, c. 1888.* **Colearne House, Auchterarder, Scotland.**

BRITISH GLASS

ABOVE *The doors of the Willow Tea Room, Glasgow, designed by Charles Rennie Mackintosh.*

At the Great Exhibition of 1851, Joseph Paxton had astonished everyone with his iron and glass Crystal Palace, which had opened up exciting opportunities as huge metal-ribbed domes and roofs of glass now became structurally possible. New commercial buildings and shops hurried to be fashionable under the influence of the Arts and Crafts Movement and the Art Nouveau style, and stained glass became an essential decorative element in building. Church building too reached a peak, demanding enormous quantities of stained glass to fill its windows, some, regrettably, of inferior quality. At the turn of the century, the vogue for stained glass was at its height; stained glass doors and transom panels became part of every middle-class house in the growing city suburbs, and studios published catalogues of standard designs.

In ecclesiastical windows two themes emerged in stained glass. The first was that produced by followers of the Arts and Crafts Movement, led by Christopher Whall, and later by his students, who included Karl Parsons, Henry Payne, and Hugh Arnold. These artists, many of them women, developed Whall's tradition of purity of colour and the highest standards of craftsmanship. The second theme was the traditional pictorial one that had been practised by Charles Eamer Kempe and carried on by Ninian Comper, and after him, by such artists as Christopher and Geoffrey Webb, and Hugh Easton.

Times, though, were changing. After the turn of the century, new thoughts in architecture – leading to less ornamentation in building – were coming to the fore, while interiors tended towards a less richly coloured and less cluttered look, with larger clear-glazed windows.

At the same time, the decrease in church building reflected changing religious and social habits. Stained glass was no longer in such demand, and this decline led to the demise of the great Victorian studios and closure of many small firms, which was sharply accelerated by the outbreak of war in 1914. In 1915, Alfred Wolmark's window in St. Mary's Church, Slough, was one of the first examples of the use of abstract designs in stained glass. This work reflected the beginnings of Cubist influence in art, but it was to take a long time before any other significant abstract stained glasswork appeared in England.

In Scotland, there was a thriving stained glass school based in Glasgow, its most notable exponent being the firm of J. & W. Guthrie. Among those who designed for them were Christopher Whall and the renowned architect Charles Rennie Mackintosh. When the latter included stained glass as part of his 1896 commission for Miss Cranston's Buchanan Street Tea

Rooms, it was Guthries who carried out the work. Mackintosh used the company extensively for his stained glass, which found more recognition in Austria, France and Germany than Britain.

A little-known part of Glasgow's rich stained glass tradition was the small, decorative painted fanlights and door-panel medallions found in the drab tenement blocks of that period, of which much, surprisingly, still survives. J. Gordon Guthrie Jr., after a family argument, left his native city in 1896 for

ABOVE *Detail of this Annunciation window, designed by Arild Rosenkranz and John La Farge and made of opalescent glass, was the first to be produced in the United States for the European market.* **Wickhambreaux Church, Kent.**

the United States, where he joined the Tiffany Studios. Later he designed for other studios, finally joining fellow Glaswegian Henry Wynd Young in New York, where they gained a considerable reputation for refined new-Gothic-style stained glass. Guthrie's work shows a skillful handling of strong colour, often combined with white, and he became one of the foremost stained glass artists of his day.

THE UNITED STATES

At the turn of the century in the United States, opalescent glass was paramount. An architectural renaissance was under way, with an emphasis towards elegant classicism using strong, clear lines.

Architects were building with marble and limestone in a grand manner for rich clients, such as the Vanderbilts, and the gentle tones of opalescent glass, its surfaces reflecting and refracting light, blended well with the new materials. The figures depicted in the windows became very grand and heroic, angels developed huge eagle-like wings, and the rich colours and swirling figural and plant forms naturally led into the restless curviform line of the Art Nouveau period. Ecclesiastical stained glass generally remained true to the Gothic tradition, although Louis Comfort Tiffany designed many of his distinctive windows for churches.

In the very early years of the 20th century, there appeared a more functional style of architecture which was concerned with space and form. The style was pioneered by Frank Lloyd Wright, who used stained glass as a screen between the inside and the outside, allowing the light and view to reach the interior of his houses. His windows have fine dominant lead lines of abstract and geometric shapes in harmony with the building, and they use colour sparingly. Much of his stained glass was made by the Linden Glass Company of Chicago, including that for perhaps his most successful architectural stained glass, in the Duna-Thomas house, built in 1904 in Springfield, Illinois. Wright's concepts were taken up in Europe, particularly in Germany, where his influence inspired a later generation of stained glass artists, including Josef Albers. It is interesting that one of the greatest American architects instigated a radical and exciting new concept in the architectural use of glass.

One of the most important stained glass studios of the 20th century was established by Charles J. Connick in Boston in 1913.

Using pure, intense colour and designs that were strong and linear, the Connick Studio was at the centre of a revival in the medieval style of stained glass craftsmanship. Inspired by the collective approach of 12th- and 13th-century artisans, the craftsmen of the Connick Studio worked together on creations that can be found in approximately 5,000 churches, schools and hospitals around the world. The studio was forced to close in 1986, but it left behind a remarkable legacy of work for future generations to marvel at.

A Break in Tradition

On the heels of the end of the First World War in 1918 came social upheaval and economic depression. It was neither a time for encouraging artistic talent nor for funding major new commissions. Viewed as a whole, the years between the wars were unremarkable for stained glass, yet it was at this time that the seeds of revolutionary ideas were sown by, amongst others, Georges Rouault in France and Jan Thorn Prikker in Germany. Suppressed by the Second World War, these seeds sprang into life in the postwar years, blossoming into a dynamic talent in the rebuilt churches and cathedrals of Europe.

A Break in Tradition

In the United States, enthusiasm for opalescent glass had already died, and a neo-Gothic style was reestablished. Here, as in Europe, an intellectual and aesthetic struggle developed to find a way out of the apparent confinement of the stereotyped tradition of pictorial ecclesiastical windows.

The release found in abstraction and symbolism was in many cases expressed by artists who were not practising Christians, and whose glass found other ways to express new purpose in the Church, such as by representing peace or calm and order in a rapidly changing world. Christian artists, too, began to express spirituality in this new art form, and a whole new concept in stained glass spread through European and American churches. However, the traditional pictorial style incorporating beautiful translucent pot-metal glass and painting has continued; in Germany, it has only barely survived, but in England and the United States it is still widely popular. In the first part of the century, though, it was in the Republic of Ireland that some of the richest of this traditional talent emerged, centred mainly in the south.

IRELAND

In Dublin in 1903, an Túr Gloine (the Tower of Glass), a cooperative-style studio similar to the Glass House in London, was founded by Edward

ABOVE *Window by Jan Thorn Prikker, in the Church of the Three Kings in Neuss, Germany, 1920's.*

Martyn and Sarah Purser. Martyn was a patron of the Abbey Theatre, Purser a successful portrait painter who, at 50, was to continue her involvement with stained glass until the grand age of 93. They chose as their manager Alfred Child, a former student of

Christopher Whall, and encouraged a medieval approach, with bold use of colour and strong careful painting. At the studios they gathered together a number of gifted artists, including Wilhelmina Geddes, Harry Clarke, Michael Healy, and Evie Hone.

Wilhelmina Geddes joined An Túr Gloine in 1912, working under the tutelage of Alfred Child. Amongst her many successful early windows was one made in 1919 for Ottawa in memory of the Duke of Connaught. In 1925, she set up her own studio in London, where, in spite of recurring poor health, she carried out some of her finest work —notably the great Te Deum War Memorial window of 1938, which Great Britain presented to the Belgian Government for St. Martin's Cathedral, Ypres.

Harry Clarke was an outstanding illustrator of books as well as a successful stained glass artist. He came from a family of church decorators and received his early training from Alfred Child at Dublin's Metropolitan School of Art. His use of rich colours in his windows is distinctive, often mixing pinks, bright greens, purples and blues. There is a certain lyrical quality about his work, such as in his window of The Nativity for the Church of Ireland at Castlelaugh, County Cork. He took immense care in his work, sometimes firing a single piece of glass several times over until he was satisfied, and

ABOVE *The east window of Eton College Chapel was executed by Evie Hone at her studio in Rathfarnham, County Dublin, 1949–52.*

never once relaxing his high standards. Probably his greatest work was the Last Judgement with the Blessed Virgin Mary and St. Patrick, for the Catholic Church of Newport, County Mayo, completed shortly before his death in 1931, at age 42.

Evie Hone was an abstract painter who became interested in stained glass on her frequent visits to France. Her first windows, made in 1934, indicate a remarkable skill. The influence of the French artist Georges Rouault and her enthusiasm for Irish medieval carvings and sculpture are apparent in many of her windows. Her most famous international commission was the large

Crucifixion and Last Supper in the east window of Eton College Chapel, which took three years to complete. She died in 1955, 11 years after An Túr Gloine had been dissolved.

AMERICAN GOTHIC

In the first part of the 20th century, ecclesiastical stained glass in the United States was largely and closely modelled on medieval glass in Europe. Outstanding examples are the many windows in the enormous neo-Gothic cathedrals of St. John the Divine in New York City, and St. Peter and St. Paul in Washington.

By the beginning of the century, the richly coloured opalescent glass landscapes in ecclesiastical architecture were anathema to a new generation of architects who rejected the mixing and abasement of different styles in Victorian building, and sought a purity based on true Gothic principles. This purity extended to the stained glass that they planned for their churches. Foremost amongst these architects was Ralph Adams Cram, whose writings and lectures were summarised in his book published in 1936, *My Life in Architecture*. Cram was appointed architect of St. John the Divine, begun in 1892, which was the largest Gothic cathedral in the world, and filled with English glass.

There was a long precedent for using English stained glass studios to make ecclesiastical windows, and this custom continued while the vogue for opalescent glass waxed and then waned. When the choir and two chapels of St. John the Divine were consecrated in 1911, the windows were from England, by Hardmans, Powell, and Clayton & Bell. They were fine examples, particularly the upper window behind the high altar of Christ in Glory by James Powell, and Clayton & Bell's St. Columba Chapel window, based on the grisaille work in York Minster, but they were Victorian in style and execution. This was perhaps the high point of Victorian ecclesiastical glass in the United States, for in that same year Cram set about creating a pure French Gothic style in St. John the Divine. He required of his stained glass that same unbroken symmetry in style and use of translucent pot-metal colour that made Chartres so much admired. His search for a suitable stained glass studio began in England, but there were already American stained glass artists who were advocating the same principles as Cram.

William Willet was a New York-born stained glass artist who had worked under John La Farge, and studied medieval glass in Europe. When he met Charles J. Connick, a newspaper cartoonist who embraced stained glass as matching his ideals and his talents, they became propagandists for a new generation of neo-Gothic stained glass artists. Others included Gordon Guthrie, originally from Glasgow, and another Scotsman, Henry Wynd Young. Willet opened his own studio in Philadelphia, and was followed by his son, Henry Lee Willet; their studio grew into one of the largest and most respected in the United States. Connick's windows often contain a predominance of blue, regarded by him and other neomedievalists as almost mystical, and his superb rose window for St. John the Divine and his colossal window in St. Vincent Ferrer in New York both testify to his belief. Another talented artist at this time was the son of Cram's partner, Wright Goodhue, who was sadly to commit suicide at the age of 26. Among his many fine windows are those in the baptistry of the Riverside Church in Manhattan. The beautiful blue background enriches the ruby glass, and strong lead lines emphasise the design. It was this church that perhaps witnessed the apogee of neo-Gothic stained glass in 1929, when a copy of the St. James's window from the clerestory at Chartres was supplied by a French studio. It was in France, though, that a new interpretation of ecclesiastical stained glass was emerging.

THE BEGINNINGS OF MODERN STAINED GLASS IN FRANCE

Ecclesiastical stained glass in France suffered considerably in both world wars. Medieval windows were removed to safety or covered up for protection, leaving the less esteemed 19th-century glass to take its chances. Inevitably, many churches and cathedrals were totally destroyed and many of those left standing lost much of their glass. Between the wars, stained glass artists banded together in craft workshops to concentrate on the restoration of the damaged glass and to exchange ideas on new glass, of which perhaps the best known was the Atelier of d'Art

ABOVE *Detail of window by Georges Braque in the Maeght Museum.*
St. Paul de Vance, France

Sacré, founded in 1919. One of the most respected studios was that of Jean Hébert-Stevens, who advocated a break with the old style, still regarded by many of the clergy as a vehicle for teaching (as it had been in medieval times). When asked to carry out a commission for the church at the Ossuaire de Douaumont near Verdun in 1927, he employed Georges Desvallières as the designer. He had been encouraged in this by the influential Dominican Father Marie-Alain Couturier, who was coauthor of the Journal, Art Sacré. In 1957, Father

ABOVE *Braques' window shows a use of bold, vivid colours and flat shapes.*
Church of St. Dominique, Varangeville, France.

RIGHT *Window by Fernand Léger in Biot, France.*

Couturier invited a number of well-known modern artists, including Georges Rouault, to make designs for the chapel of Notre-Dame-de-Toute-Grace at Assy in Haute-Savoie. The result was a startling, if controversial, new interpretation of religious stained glass, though not entirely successful because of the differing styles. Father Couturier was heavily criticised for turning the church into an exhibition of modern profane art, but after he died in 1954, Marc Chagall was commissioned to make further designs for the baptistry windows.

The experience at Assy was the beginning of abstract art in religious stained glass. It is interesting that the International Exhibition of that same year was dominated by the work of the traditional studios, whose detailed figures of saints in the new windows for the cathedral of Notre-Dame were already being regarded as dated and dull. However, at the 1939 Exposition des Arts Décoratifs at the Petit Palais, work by such new modern artists as Jean Bazaine, Roger Bissiers, and Francis Gruber was widely acclaimed.

RIGHT *A window by Jean Cocteau in St. Maximin.*
Metz, France.

Marc Chagall

Marc Chagall was 70 years old when his first stained glass windows were installed at Assy in 1957.

ABOVE *A memorial window to Sarah D'Avigdor-Goldsmid – one of 12 windows designed by Marc Chagall and executed by Charles and Brigitte Marcq of the Atelier Jacques Simon in Reims for All Saints Church, Tudeley, Kent.*

This remarkable man stands independently of other stained glass artists working after the war, and his unique contributions to the art made a dramatic and lasting impact.

Born Moyshe Shagall in 1877 in Russia, he left his hometown and set off for Paris in 1911, carrying with him all the mysticism and influence of the icons that he must have seen in his Russian upbringing. In Paris, he was influenced by Cubism and the Impressionist painters, particularly Gauguin and van Gogh. He returned to Russia in 1914 to marry his childhood sweetheart, Bella, and did not return to Paris until 1923, where his painting, ceramic decoration, and lithographs, found wide acclaim. His swirling dreamlike imagery resulted from his view of life – 'I am a mystic. I don't go to church or to the synagogue. For me working is praying'.

Following Assy, his next important commission was for the cathedral at Metz between 1960 and 1965. Here, as in all his windows, the problem of translating his work into glass was entrusted to Charles and Brigitte Marcq in Reims. The Marcqs carefully and laboriously met his colour requirements and by painting, aciding and etching, they faithfully created his floating forms and bold lines in glass, paint and lead. In 1962, he produced 12 windows for the Hadassah Medical Centre in Jerusalem, where, to avoid portraying the human figure (forbidden in Judaic art), he used symbols and animals with human characteristics. His window for the

United Nations in memory of Dag Hammarskjöld is an essay in blue, a favorite color of his, which he used again in his beautiful memorial window in All Saints Church, Tudeley, Kent, to Sarah d'Avigdor-Goldsmid, who was drowned in a sailing accident.

ABOVE *A memorial window to Dag Hammarskjöld, former Secretary-General of the United Nations, designed by Marc Chagall for the United Nations building in New York. It is predominantely blue and strewn with coloured images representing peace.*

Jan Thorn Prikker

Thorn Prikker was Dutch by birth, but worked and taught in Germany and was, like his counterparts in France, principally an abstract painter.

His work in stained glass uses dynamic elements in simplified pictorial form, sometimes, as in his panel Orange of 1931, limited to one plane. Similar experiments in glass grew from the influential Bauhaus school, where Theo Van Doesburg, Paul Klee and Josef Albers were involved with its stained glass department (unfortunately, little of their work survived the war). Thorn Prikker's work created enormous interest in a new generation of German stained-glass artists who carried their work into the 1950s, principally Anton Wendling, Heinrich Camperdonk, and Georg Meistermann. Like the French craftsmen, Meistermann was veering away from figurative glass. His work was to reach its peak with his windows in the Church of St. Maria-im-Kapital, where his

use of paint was minimal and the composition of the windows displayed a great freedom of style. His then-revolutionary windows in 1938 for the Church of St. Engelbert at Solingen in the Ruhr were sadly destroyed in the war.

Anton Wendling made his home before the war in Aachen, where in 1949 he designed huge abstract windows in geometric patterns for the choir in Aachen Cathedral. His windows tend to comprise a repeating geometric pattern, often referred to as tiered coloured masonry. In 1947, when teaching at the Technical University, he engaged as his assistant a young artist named Ludwig Schaffrath, who was to be one of the greatest post-war stained glass artists in Europe.

LEFT *Blue opalescent glass by Johannes Schreiter, in the Johannesbund Chapel in Leutesdorf, West Germany.*

John Piper

Apart from Alfred Wolmark's early experiment in abstract composition in 1915 at St. Mary's, Slough, commissioned by Mr. Ellerman of Ellerman's Embrocation fame, England between the wars kept safely to its pictorial painterly tradition in stained glass.

The work of A.K. Nicholson, Martin Travers, and Hugh Easton was in this tradition, though individual in style, as was that of Christopher Webb, whose post-war Shakespeare window in Southwark Cathedral is much admired. At the end of the war, although many churches in southern England had been damaged by bombing, there was nothing like the opportunity for new commissions that existed in Germany. Much of the new glass looked backward, and although generally of high quality, owed nothing to the contemporary work then being carried out on the Continent.

LEFT *Window in the Basilika of St. Gereon, Cologne, by Georg Meistermann.*

It was the rebuilding of Coventry Cathedral and the new Roman Catholic Cathedral in Liverpool that revolutionized stained glass in England.

Destroyed by bombing during the war, Coventry Cathedral was rebuilt by the architect Sir Basil Spence, using concrete and glass with the new

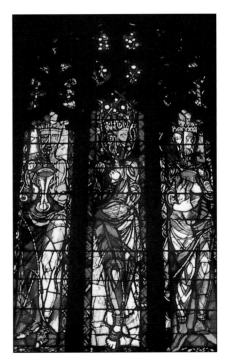

ABOVE *One of the three Gothic-style windows in Oundle Chapel, Northamptonshire. They were John Piper's first stained glass commission and represent the nine aspects of Christ. They were executed by Patric Reyntiens in 1955.*

building linked to the remains of the old. The nave windows – 70 in all – were dangled to catch the southern light and visible in their entirety only from the altar end. Designed by Lawrence Lee, Geoffrey Clarke and Keith New, they represent, through symbolic use of colour, the relationship between God and Man at different stages in Man's life. They were a radical break with tradition, but it was the huge curved window in the baptistry by John Piper that created the greatest controversy when the cathedral was consecrated in 1962, and is now accepted as a landmark in British stained-glass design. A great sunburst of colour reaching from floor to ceiling, the window symbolizes the light of the Holy Spirit breaking through into the world. Surrounding the central blaze of yellow and white rectangles are abstract patterns in purples, blues, reds, greens, browns, ochres and greys. More in the French than the English tradition, John Piper the artist made the design and the cartoon, but left the interpretation into glass to Patrick Reyntiens.

Their earliest windows, installed in Oundle School Chapel in 1956, of nine symbolic knights in vivid colour and with strong curvilinear painting and leading, are still considered by many to be amongst their best work, as well as a watershed in English stained glass. Following Coventry, Piper and

ABOVE *This Romanesque-style composition by John Piper and Patrick Reyntiens portrays the Adoration of the Magi, flanked by trumpeting angels with two pagan monsters beneath their feet. Below are Adam and Eve, and on the right, The Last Supper.*
Robinson College, Cambridge, 1982.

Reyntiens were given the commission for the great lantern tower in Liverpool Cathedral (1963–67), the abstract design in *dalle de verre* crowns the inside of the cathedral by day, and, when lit at night, it is like a spectacular lighthouse of colour from the outside. Amongst their many successful later works are the chancel windows for the chapel of Robinson College, Cambridge. Other English artists working at this time included Brian Thomas, Margaret Traherne, Francis Skeat, Keith New and Arthur Buss, who designed the enormous heraldic rose window at Lancing College in Sussex, the largest built in Europe since the Reformation.

Glossary

Antique glass: A term referring to mouth-blown flat glass. It is not as its name implies – "aged" or old. Colours range from deep rich tones to pale tints and each piece may be different with striations and texture and non-uniform in thickness. Within this category are also plain, seedy, streaky, reamy and flashed antique.

Beading: Melting enough solder to form a "bead" or rounded seam over copper foil.

Bevels: Shapes of glass with angles ground into the edges and polished.

Breaking Pliers: An aid to breaking glass along the score line.

Carborundum Stone: A hand tool for sanding or smoothing the edges of glass.

Cartoon: The working drawing or design of a window showing all the lead widths and cut lines that are to be followed. Copies of this "original" would be made.

Cathedral Glass: A machine-made transparent glass.

Cementing: The process of forcing lead light cement into gaps between the lead and glass leaving the panel watertight and strong.

Copper Foil: A variety of different widths of copper foil with an adhesive backing applied to pieces of glass for bonding together. Commonly used in lamp shades and internal or intricate window panels and useful for sculptural or three-dimensional objects.

Cut Line: The line marked on the cartoon depicting where to cut the glass.

Cutting Square: Specialized ruler used as a guide for cutting right angles.

Etching: The process of applying hydrofluoric acid to the surface of the glass either to remove the top layer of flashed glass or as a decorative technique on clear glass.

Fid: Plastic multipurpose instrument used for opening lead cames and rubbing down copper foil onto the glass.

Firing: A process requiring a kiln into which glass that has been painted is "fired."

Flashed Glass: A glass of one colour that has a thin layer of another colour on top. The base glass can either be clear (white) or coloured. The surface colour can be etched or sandblasted away to reveal the base glass.

Flux: A chemical that allows solder to flow onto the surface of the metals to be joined.

Fluxing: Applying a liquid flux to copper foil or lead before soldering.

Fusing: The art of melting one glass directly onto another in a kiln.

Foiling: The process of wrapping copper foil around the edges of glass.

Glass Cutter: A hand tool used for scoring glass.

Glass Nuggets: Irregular rounded pieces of thick

coloured glass in various colours and sizes.

Grinding Machine: Electrically powered machine with a rotating wheel to grind pieces of glass into shapes.

Grozing: The method of removing fine shards and slivers from the edges of glass.

Grozier Pliers: Pliers with a narrow head and fine teeth for grozing glass.

Horseshoe Nails: Flat-sided nails used to stabilise the lead cames during the leading process.

Kiln: A special oven made of firebrick powered by gas or electricity.

Laminated Glass: Two layers of glass bonded together by a resin.

Lathe: Tool used to open the lead channels.

Lead Came: Lengths of lead with channels on either side to accommodate glass. Used mainly for windows and more durable than copper foil. Available in many different widths.

Lead Knife: Used to cut through lead came. Came cutters or lead snips are also available for this purpose.

Lead Stretcher: A special vice or clamp for holding down lead on a bench or table while it is pulled by hand from the other end.

Leading: The technique of assembling a window or panel using lead cames to hold the glass together.

Matting: A term for creating shading tones when painting on glass. Different implements are used to remove the initial application of paint, thereby creating a variety of effects and textures.

Mouth-blown glass: Made by blowing molten glass into a "muff" or cylindrical bubble. The ends are then cut leaving a cylinder shape. A cut is made on the side of the glass and placed back in the kiln and it will fold out into a piece of flat glass.

Opalescent Glass: Opaque or non-transparent glass associated with "Tiffany-style" lampshades.

Generally machine-made.

Oxidation: A condition that will occur on lead and copper foil if they are exposed to the atmosphere for too long before soldering. A rub with wire wool or a wirebrush is used before soldering to remove.

Paint: A black-brown vitreous enamel used with special brushes for decorating glass that is then "fired" in a kiln and fuses the paint to the surface of the glass.

Pattern Scissors: These come in at least two sizes. They are for making templates and will create a double cut to allow for the width of the heart of the lead. There are also pattern scissors for cutting copper foil templates.

Resist: An adhesive-backed material such as vinyl that is used to "mask" or protect select areas of glass when sandblasting or etching.

Rolled Glass: Refers to machine-made flat glass that, as its name implies, is made by molten glass passing through two parallel rollers.

Roundels: Hand-spun or machine-pressed circles of glass with smooth finished edges. Available in various sizes and colours.

Running Pliers: Special pliers that can be used for breaking a straight score on long, narrow strips of glass.

Sandblasting: A technique where sand projected by a compressor abrades the surface of the glass. Sandblasting can penetrate deeply and can "carve" the surface of thick glass.

Score: The fine fracture line created on the surface of glass with the wheel of a glass cutter.

Scoring: The process of applying pressure and moving the glass cutter over the surface of the glass to produce a light fracture.

Semiantique glass: Machine-made flat glass with little movement but brilliant colours.

Silver Stain: Applied like glass paint, this substance contains silver nitrate that will colour glass when fired. During firing the stain penetrates the glass. It produces shades of yellow through to amber.

Solder: A mixture of tin and lead used to bend lead cames and copper foil together; 50:50 or 40:60 generally used.

Soldering Iron: Tool used for melting solder.

Tallow: Wax candle used to rub on the joints of lead before soldering.

Tapping: A technique that assists the breaking of glass by using the ball end of a cutter. The glass is tapped from underneath.

Template: Paper or cardboard shape used to mark out a pattern on the glass prior to scoring.

Tinning: Melting a flat coating of solder over copper foil.

Tracing: Painting outlines on glass with trace paint.

Bibliography

The following books and publications explore in more detail the personalities and historical aspects of stained glass covered in this book.

Brisac, Catherine, *A Thousand Years of Stained Glass*, Chartwell Books Inc., 1984

Chieffo Raguin, Virgina, *The History of Stained Glass: The Art of Light— Medieval to Contemporary*, 2003

Cowen, Painton, *Rose Windows*, Thames and Hudson, 1978

Duncan, Alistair, *Master Works of Louis Comfort Tiffany*, Thames and Hudson Ltd.,1989

Gordon Bowe, Nichola, *The Life and Work of Harry Clarke*, Irish Academic Press, 1989

Lillich, Meredith P., *The Armor of Light: Stained Glass in Western France 1250-1325*, University of California Press, 1994

Osborne, June, *John Piper and Stained Glass*, Thames and Hudson, 1997

Osborne, June, *Stained Glass in England*, Muller, 1981

Sloan, Julie L., *Conservation of Stained Glass in America*, Art and Architecture, 1995

Sloan, Julie L., *Light Screens: The Leaded Glass of Frank Lloyd Wright*, Rizzoli International, 2001

Schutz, Bernhard, *Great Cathedrals*, Harry N. Abrams, Inc., 2002

Williamson, Paul, *Mediaeval and Renaissance Stained Glass in the Victoria and Albert Museum*, V.& A publications, 2003

The Journal of Stained Glass (American Issue), Published by British Society of Master Glass Painters (front cover features a detail of Charles J. Connick's Tolerence window, 1938, in the north transept of Heinz Memorial Chapel, Pittsburgh. Also includes contributions on the history of American Stained Glass, research, methodology and contemporary practice.)

The following publications are available from the Connick Foundation (*www.cjconnick.org/publications*)

Cormack, Peter, *The Stained Glass Work of Christopher Whall (1849-1924)*, 1999

Cormack, Peter, *Vol.XXVII Journal of Stained Glass. American Issue (2004)*, (includes articles: Charles J. Connick and the Arts and Crafts philosophy of stained glass)

Skinner, Orin E., *Stained Glass Tours: Boston*

Stained Glass Association of America produces the *Stained Glass Quartlerly*, which features full-colour articles about historical and contemporary installations that will show you what others are doing in the field.
(*e-mail quarterly@sgaaonline.com*)

INDEX